REBUILDING YOUR BROKEN WALL

WITH OVER 400 UNCOMMON PRAYERS

BY

Daramola Joel Odunayo

Tel: 08033275896, 07028206482

ISBN: 9798369636596

Published by

CHRIST THE REDEEMER'S MINISTRIES

1-9, Redemption Way, P.M.B. 1088, Ebute Metta, Lagos, Nigeria.

Unless otherwise stated, all scriptural quotation are from the Authorized King James Version of the Holy Bible.

Printed in Nigeria by: **CRM PRESS**

KM 46 Lagos-Ibadan Expressway, CRM Shopping Complex,

Back of Old Auditorium, Redemption Camp,

Tel: 08077833792, 08069452037

E-mail: crmpress@yahoo.com

TABLE OF CONTENT

PREAMBLE

He that hath no rule over his own spirit is like a city that is broken down, and without walls. And so, it is in extreme danger. Proverbs 25:28

Let every man take heed how he builds. For other foundation can no man lay than that is laid which is Jesus Christ. 1 Corinthians 3:10-17

Rebuilding your broken walls means several things and we need to understand these few things:

What the spiritual meaning of wall, perimeter, fence or compound is.

What can make your spiritual wall break?

What is the danger of broken wall or being fenceless?

Like Nehemiah, do you have burden for your people?

You need favour from the king to make things happen for his people.

For every level there are devils; remember that your success will grieve Sanballat and Tobiah incarnates.

What are the processes of rebuilding broken wall?

Why many start to build or rebuild and unable to complete it.

Dealing with intruder who benefits in broken wall, and their friends.

Getting resources to rebuild without compromise.

Reconciling with God and breaking the curses.

The objectives of this book are:

To examine Nehemiah's reaction to the news concerning Jerusalem.

To highlight "broken walls" in Christendom today and how we should react to them.

To discuss the strategies used by the enemies to hinder the rebuilding of broken walls.

To identify the strategies we can put up to rebuild the broken walls.

To discuss the blessings in rebuilding the broken walls.

THE AGONY OF A BROKEN WALL(Nehemiah 1:2-7)

Today, walls that once provided protection against the enemy's schemes are crumbling all around us—in our families, our churches, and our culture. Today, more than ever, God is calling His people to be men and women who, like Nehemiah, will trust Him with their lives and work to repair the damage before it is too late.

Our Nation is filled with broken walls. The walls of human morality have fallen. The wall of the Christian family have fallen. The walls of peace are crumbling all around us. The walls of our military might have been weaken by exploitation and evil association. The walls of prayerfulness have been replaced by secularism and humanism. Yet God is still calling a people at this very hour to rebuild broken walls.

What do you do when the devastatingly unexpected happens?

"But you also said that no matter how far away we were, we could turn to you and start obeying your laws. Then you would bring us back to the place where you have chosen to be worshiped." Nehemiah 1:9 (CEV)

The question is: what is our response as Christians to a broken and torn apart world? Or at a deeper level: what is God's response to such a world? From the bible we know what God's response is: wholeness, restoration, re-union and redemption [Is. 61, 65:17-25, Rom. 8:18-21, Eph. 1:9-10, Col. 1:15-23, Rev. 21]. That's why Jesus died on the cross: to make everything new. And God's response should exactly be our response: God wants you to extend His 'wholeness' into a broken and torn apart world [Micah 6:8].

Nehemiah is the last of the historical books in the Old Testament and tells us how Nehemiah restored the broken wall of Jerusalem. He was a man who took God's wholeness and restoration into a broken and torn apart nation.

The Jews, as prophesied, were in captivity and while there, most of them had assured Babylonia as their home, and were contented as slaves and servants. While in captivity Nehemiah found himself in the palace, i.e. close to the authority. Despite the comfort that the Palace offered, he had a yearning and compassion for his home and was not in any way derailed or overtaken by the comfort of the Palace. To show his overwhelming passion, he asked after the state of his beloved city Jerusalem when the opportunity showed up. When Nehemiah Learnt that his people were in great affliction and the walls of Jerusalem were in ruins, he mourned and rose to the challenge.

In his reaction, he wept, mourned, fasted and prayed; he reminded God that he was a covenant-keeping God. He prayed for God's mercies and was persistent in his prayers (twice- day and night). He also confessed not only his personal sins, but that of his nation. His deep sorrow for his wasted land was not hidden. He knew the right request to make and was not self-centered, but was after the fulfillment of God's purpose. He later got the King's authority to go to Jerusalem to rebuild the broken walls and he restored the people spiritually. It must be noted that Nehemiah knew God as his God, based on personal encounter (Neh. 1: 8).

One of the things that could be learnt from the experience of Nehemiah is that, he kept and meditated on what God had put in his heart: (Neh. 1:12). He also arose and did something by taking appropriate actions and was not a wishful thinker. Lastly, he was able to identify those of like minds to which he revealed God's purpose and was able to resist the enemy of his vision. In his commitment to God, he exhibited leadership qualities that led to the rebuilding of the walls of Jerusalem in 52 days; He was a man of faith and determination.

WHO OR WHAT CAN COLLAPSE THE WALL?

The English word 'wall' is derived from the Latin, vallus meaning 'a stake' or 'post' and designated the wood-stake and earth palisade which formed the outer edge of a fortification. Walls have traditionally been built for defense, privacy, and to protect the people of a certain region from the influence or perceived danger posed by outsiders. Thus, a wall is to protect from the enemy, give security to those on the inside. It is not just to surround a city but, rather, mark a territorial boundary.

We need walls:

The wall of salvation – John 3:16 – It keeps us from perishing.

The wall of holiness – 1st Pet. 1:15-16. (15: but as He who called you is holy, you also be holy in all your conduct, 16: because it is written, “Be holy, for I am holy.”)

The wall of separation – 2nd Cor. 6:16-17 – 16And what agreement has the temple of God with idols? For you are the temple of the living God. As God has said: “I will dwell in them and walk among them. I will be their God, and they shall be My people.” 17 “Therefore come out from among them and be separate,” says the Lord. “Do not touch what is unclean, and I will receive you.” (see also verses 11-15)

The wall of God’s Word – Prov. 29:18 - Where there is no vision, the people perish: but he that keepeth the law, happy is he.

Foundational Problem.

This is what I mean by that: When the walk with the Lord is not taken seriously, salvation experience becomes a routine, personal relationship with God in His word and fellowship become remote, the foundation becomes faulty. Today, because from the time one responded to the altar call, the new life is treated with levity and without seriousness; the sinner’s prayer is said mostly as a matter of formality, the sinner has no value for the new life he has found hence it is easy to compromise. Since he is not rooted in the word, he falls easily to all sorts of trials and temptation, and become an easy prey to the devil.

The Sin Problem/Careless Living

Due to the poor foundation, sin is not seen as seen rather, it is treated with levity and accommodated. Brethren often make excuse for their short comings by covering, instead of renting their hearts before God and ask for his mercy; they even point at other presumed men of God doing worst things.

When telling a little lie is not considered a sin, skipping the time for quiet time with God is nothing, compromising our stand in the face of worldly profits and gain is nothing to fuse about, then the wall gets cracking.

Lack of Power

The eyes of God are too pure behold sin (Habakkuk 1:13). Due to the sin issue discussed above, the presence and power of God as it was mightily experienced by the early church and in the 1970's to 1980 is absent from many today's church.

Lack of Voice/Relevance in the Nation's Affairs

In scriptures, due to the mighty presence and power of God that was in the Church, its relevance in national matters could not be relegated to the background. The prophets and the priests were feared, obeyed as they directed the affairs of the nations. Kings could entrust their decision and actions based on the advice of the men of God as such advice, instructions and prophesies were most reliable and dependable. Today, much is left to be desired in this regard concerning the life of many children of God.

Fear

When the fear of man, circumstances and systems and practices take over the fear of God, the wall gets broken. Fear brings torment as long as it not of God (1 John 4:18).When that happens, the wall of defence for a believer becomes weaken and may fall if not overcome.

STEPS TO REBUILD

The broken walls can be diverse. There are broken walls martially. Some are broken walls in the area of finance, some it is self esteem, and countless others. Whichever way, the broken walls would always concern you, God and others (as we do not live for self only).

Therefore, rebuilding the broken walls of our lives can be approached generally using these steps:

Nehemiah did not set out to rebuild the broken walls by his own strength. Do not set out to rebuild the broken walls of your live by your strength. Ps. 60:11; Prov. 3:5-6.

We must base the rebuilding of our broken walls upon the word of God and Godly principles, as there can be no rebuilding of broken walls outside God. Prov. 4:20-21

We must, like Nehemiah realize we have our broken walls and repent sincerely and genuinely. Sin must not be toiled with and we must live an exemplary life as Christians. 1 John 1:9-10.

We must have at the back of our mind that heaven is an individual race and not a congregational race. We must therefore seek to know God for ourselves individually as we try to help as many as we can to do the same.

Just as Nehemiah set up a watch, day and night, the believer is to be watchful and vigilant. (Neh. 4:9, 1Pet 5:8).

We as believers must stand out for what we believe at all times even if it means standing alone. To rebuild our broken walls, we must know and carry with us the consciousness that we are light to brighten the dark world as we point the world to Christ, and that we are salt to sweeten, preserve and give taste to our world. The believer must know he is Jesus that men see today. Matt.5:13-16.

The place of holy living is a major strategy to rebuild our broken walls. There must be a determination to live for Christ at all times, in all situations.

DEALING WITH INTERNAL ENEMIES

The devil is the arch enemy of God's children. He does not come physically to commit havoc in and against you, but he uses different ways, part of which is to locate the areas of your weakness or frailty, I mean mechanism within you without any interference from outside yourself.

For us, it may come in the form of habits, interests, or attitude:

laziness in prayers,

laziness in the study of God's word,

decreased enthusiasm in fellowship with the brethren,

procrastination,

treating God's instruction with levity, etc.

The main aim of all these is to make the believer complacent and then to compromise his faith and eventually miss heaven. But like Nehemiah and his workers who are battle-ready as they worked, today's Christian should put aside all sorts of distractions and run the heavenly race with determination to make it amidst all oppositions. Philippians 4:8-9; 2 Peter 1:5-11.

DEALING WITH THE EXTERNAL ENEMIES

Dealing with the external enemies is dealing with any force that wages war against our peace, our faith and our stand in God from around us, from friends, family members, co-workers, etc. Satan uses his demons and human agents. For Nehemiah, they came in form of Sanballat and Tobiah and a host of other adversaries that came along. They wore them out, mocked them and despised their efforts.

Notice the opposition that Nehemiah faced and the victories that he won.

I. Ridicule (Neh. 4: 1-6)

God's people always have enemies. In this case, they were

Sanballat, a government official in Samaria; Tobiah, the Ammonite; and Geshem, an Arabian were three wicked men outside the nation of Israel.In fact, the Ammonites were definite enemies of the Jews (Deut. 23:3-4).Their first weapon was ridicule; they mocked the "feeble Jews" openly before the leaders of Samaria. Satan is a mocker (Luke 22:63; 23:35-37). Ridicule is a device used by ignorant people who are filled with jealousy.

How did Nehemiah answer them? He prayed to his God! His concern was only for the glory of God and the testimony of the nation. Satan would have loved to see Nehemiah leave the wall and get involved in a dispute with Sanballat, but Nehemiah did not fall into Satan's trap. Never allow ridicule to stop your ministry.

II. Force (Neh. 4:7-9)

What Satan cannot accomplish by deceit he attempts to do by force.It is amazing how the devil seems to have no manpower shortage. They were two enemies in Neh.2: 10, three enemies in Neh.2:19, and a whole multitude in Neh.4:7.In facing these enemies, he prayed and set a watch. "Watch and pray!" is a repeated admonition in the New Testament. Note that Nehemiah did not depend on prayer alone; he also set a watch.

III. Discouragement (Neh. 4: 10)

Satan followed this same tactic in Acts 5-6 when he used Ananias and Sapphira and the complaining widows inside the fellowship of the church.He also used Judas inside the ranks of the apostles.How discouraged the workers were, with all that rubbish on the inside of the city and the danger lurking on the outside. We do not read that Nehemiah paid much attention to their complaint, though; he kept on building, watching, and praying.

IV. Fear (Neh. 4:11-23)

Fear and faith can never abide in the same heart. In Neh. 4:11, we have a rumor the enemy stated that their armies would suddenly invade Jerusalem.The Jews living outside the city heard this report and carried it to Nehemiah ten different times.

In response to this, Nehemiah set the guard on the walls and encouraged the people not to fear, though the work stopped in Neh. 4:13 to 15-exactly what the enemy wanted. Nehemiah saw the folly of this plan, so he put the workers back on the job, a weapon in one hand and a tool in the other.He also set a special watch with trumpets (v. 19-20), but he did not allow the work to stop.

These Jews are wonderful examples of what a Christian worker ought to be: they had a mind to work (4:6), a heart to pray (4:9), an eye to watch (4:9), and an ear to hear (4:20).

V. Selfishness (5)

Nehemiah was angry (v. 6) because his people were so spiritually backslidden as to rob one another. He saw it not as an economic problem, but as a spiritual problem. He consulted with his own heart (v. 7) and certainly prayed to God for wisdom.Then he rebuked the people (vv. 7-11), reminding them of God's goodness to their nation. "We have been set free by the Lord," he argued, "will you now put one another in bondage again?"

VI. Guile (6:1-4) (deceptiveness, fraudulence or manipulation)

The people went back to work, and so did the enemy. This time Sanballat and his men aimed their attacks on Nehemiah the leader.Many of God's people will never realize here on earth the special temptations and testing God's servants face day after day. Spiritual leadership is a costly thing – family, workplace, church, verywhere.

SETTING UP YOUR GATES AND GATE KEEPERS

The Hebrew names of these gates have great significance. I would like to quickly describe these for your own edification, and we can draw the lesson from each at the same time.

Sheep Gate

The Sheep Gate, of course, signifies the Lamb of God, whose blood was shed on the cross for us, and, therefore, it reveals the principle of the cross.

Fish Gate

"And Jesus said to them, "Follow me, and I will make you become fishers of men." (Mark 1:17)

This suggests the witness of a Christian. If you can never say a word for Christ, if there is never any witness in your life, then this wall is broken and the Fish Gate needs to be built again.

Old Gate

Well, I suggest that it represents truth. In many Christians' lives this gate is broken down — they are no longer resting upon truth. Truth is always old, and it is upon old things that everything new must rest.

Dung Gate

This is the place through which all the refuse of the city was carried; all the garbage, all the filth was carried. It was taken out through the Dung Gate. And my friend, if you do not have a dung gate in your life, you're in bad shape because all the refuse in your life is accumulated and it will make you smell in the sight of God and man.

Valley Gate

This suggests the place of humility. It is the place of lowliness of mind and humbleness of heart. God has said in every page of Scripture that he is against the pride of men.

Fountain Gate

It speaks of the Holy Spirit, which is the river of life in us — the flowing of the Spirit of God in our lives, to enable us to obey his will and his word.

Water Gate

Water is always a symbol of the word of God. The interesting thing about this Water Gate is that it did not need to be repaired. Evidently it was the only part of the wall that was still standing.

East Gate

The East Gate faced the rising sun, and is the gate of hope.

It is the gate of anticipation of what is yet to come when all the trials of life and all the struggles of earth will end and the glorious new sun will rise on the new day of God.

Horse Gate

“For we do not wrestle against flesh and blood, but against the rulers, against the authorities, against the cosmic powers over this present darkness, against the spiritual forces of evil in the heavenly places.” (Ephesians 6:12)

The horse in scripture is a symbol of warfare or, in this case, the need to do battle against the forces of darkness.

Master Gate or, literally, the “examination gate.”

We need to sit and take a look at ourselves every now and then — to stop and re-evaluate what we are doing.

THANKSGIVING

Psalms 136 :1-26.

Thanksgiving is an act of worshipping God. A heart of Thanksgiving is a heart of submission, love and a heart that gives glory to God (Luke 17:11-19). The life that gives thanks to God is always different from the life of an unbeliever. Don't take anything in life as your right. It is a privilege from God. Anytime you see yourself taking the privilege of God as your right, it means you are unthankful. Unthankful spirit is a sign of the end time.

Giving to God is an act of showing gratitude. Giving is like a sacrifice. Giving makes you better. Anything given to God must be given to him with submission and humility (Genesis 4:1-7). Don't be arrogant when you are giving to God, because you did not bring anything to this world, neither will you take anything back.

Anytime you see yourself giving with pride, you are giving to the devil. The hand of God can never work in your life if you are robbing God. There are places in life you can never get to, but your giving will take you there. Any giving that does not touch you, is not a giving. It has to touch you to touch God. Never look at God as a thief. There is nothing you give to God that can make you bigger than Him. Your tithe is a sign of Thanksgiving and gratitude to God. This time around, offer your thanks to God that He answers all your prayers, that He has rebuilt the broken walls of your life.

FIRST DIVISION: THANKSGIVING AND GRATITUDE

INSTRUCTIONS

Study the Bible passages, sing the Hymns, praise the Lord throughout the twenty-one days.

During the21days, you are expected to pray at least 60 minutes (1-hour) daily. You can divide it into 2 or 3 that is 30minutes or 20 minutes.

Observe a compulsory one hour vigil between 11:30 to after midnight or 1:00 am daily. Pray for yourself, your sources of income, our Church to wake up from her spiritual slumber, our community for total recovery from demonic caretaker and revival; pray for our Pastors and leaders.

If you are not born again or you are not sure you are born again, pray these prayers before continuing: "O! Lord my father, I come unto you as a wretched sinner, have mercy on me, forgive me all of all my sins. Make me your child as from today. Write my name in the book of Life. Wash me clean with the blood of Jesus. Thank you my father for saving my soul. I declare that I am born again to the glory of God in the name of Jesus (John 3 v 16)

If you are discouraged, you are backsliding, perhaps your past is hunting you, receive the Grace of the Lord to repent of your past sins/habits now.

Renounce them, ask God to take away from you any strange urge or taste for evil/defilement. Then ask the Holy Spirit to strengthen your inner man. (Ephesians 3 v 16)

You must pray and remain Holy always? - Ps. 55 v 16; 17; Ps. 34 v 15 & 17; Ps. 65 v 2; 1 Pet. 1 v 15

SECTION ONE (1)

Thanksgiving

1 Thessalonians 5:18, Psalm 100, Psalm 103.

Appreciation should be given to God before any requests are tabled to Him. Praises to God in the mouth of God's people is comely, befitting and very desirable. Make up your mind to praise Him this first day of the prayer and fasting.

Father, thank you for your goodness and mercy.

Father, thank you for yet another corporate prayer and fasting time in your church

Father, thank you for counting me worthy to be part this year.

Father, let all my thanksgiving be acceptable to you.

Father, let my prayers be directed by your spirit. Lead me to praise in every matter of my life.

Prophetic Declarations

Psalms 30:11-12 The Lord will give you and your family UNENDING OVERLAPPING TURNAROUND TESTIMONIES in all areas of life this new year in Jesus name. You will experience a glorious new beginning of JOY, FAVOUR and BLESSINGS in Jesus name. You will not SORROW throughout this New Year and God will ACCELERATE your PROGRESS in Jesus name. Welcome to your year of a NEW DAWN. Remain BLESSED for LIFE and enjoy the rest of the year.

SECTION TWO (2):

Intense Praise And Worship

Thank God for being God. Gen 17:1

Thank God for your life and for what God is doing through you. Ps. 124

Thank God for creating this beautiful world. Gen 1:1-31

Prophetic Declarations

And he closed the book, and he gave it again to the minister, and sat down. And the eyes of all them that were in the synagogue were fastened on him (Luke 4:20)

Upon you today where others are being rejected and frustrated, your own life and destiny shall command divine attractions and progress, in the mighty name of Jesus Christ.

Every handwriting of Satan upon your life, business and career shall be nullified by the blood of the lamb, in the mighty name of Jesus Christ.

SECTION THREE (3):

Thank God for sustaining us through the days of fasting and Prayer.

Thank God for answered prayers

Thank God for granting us the strength to grow through the fast. I Chronicles 16:34, Psalm 18:46-50

Thank you God for your mercy on your church. Rom. 9: 15-16.

Prophetic Declarations

And the angel came in unto her, and said, Hail, thou that art highly favoured, the Lord is with thee: blessed art thou among women (Luke 1:28)

Today the angels of good news will locate your habitations to register your turn for a turn around, in the mighty name of Jesus Christ

your strength shall be renewed by the precious blood of the lamb, in the mighty name of Jesus Christ.

SECTION FOUR (4):

Give thanks "In everything."

Thank God for making a year of surprise

Let us thank God for not allowing civil war to tear our country apart.

Let us thank God for not allowing hunger and famine in our country.

Let us bless the name of Jehovah God for his protection last year. Ps 124:1-end

Prophetic Declarations

What do ye imagine against the LORD? He will make an utter end: affliction shall not rise up the second time (Nahum 1:9)

God will surely deliver you from every affliction that hindered your ancestors from fulfilling their destinies, in the mighty name of Jesus.

Your hands shall find rest in every area of your finances, in the mighty name of Jesus.

SECTION FIVE (5):

Thanksgiving further commits God to you and your affairs.

He who knows how to think will know how to thank. Think of all God's goodness to you and all that are yours and continue to appreciate Him. Psalms 136. Let your thanksgiving flow from the heart.

Father, I thank you for keeping me, my family and all that pertain to me. Psalm 34:1-6

Thank you O' Lord for bringing me into this year. Job 33:18
Thank you Father for keeping me and all that are mine this year. Psalm 16:5-6

Thank you Father for your mercies on my life and family. Lamentations 3:22

Prophetic Declarations

Thou shalt arise, and have mercy upon Zion: for the time to favour her, yea, the set time, is come (Psalm 102:13)

as you wake up this morning, your angels shall bring you in contact with supernatural favour with God and with man, in the mighty name of Jesus.

Angels of God shall bring you in contact with your covenant helpers, in the mighty name of Jesus.

SECTION SIX (6):

1. Thank God for sustaining us through the days of fasting and Prayer.
2. Thank God for answered prayers
3. Thank God for granting us the strength to grow through the 50 days fast.

1 Chronicles 16:34, Psalm 18:46-50

Prophetic Declarations

The woman then left her waterpot, and went her way into the city, and saith to the men, Come; see a man, which told me all things that ever I did: is not this the Christ?

(John 4:28-29)

today, the lord will introduce you and the gift of God at work in you to people and organisations that matters to your destiny in life, in the mighty name of Jesus.

God will destroy the network of Satan and all his agents around your life, in the mighty name of Jesus Christ.

SECTION SEVEN (7):

Thanksgiving

Thank God for His mercy on you and yours Rom. 9: 15-16

Thank God for what He is doing in our nation.

Thank God for His mercy all over the world.

Prophetic Declarations

So shall they fear the name of the LORD from the west, and his glory from the rising of the sun. When the enemy shall come in like a flood, the Spirit of the LORD shall lift up a standard against him (Isaiah 59:19)

whenever the devil stands to afflict you, the spirit of the lord shall lift up a standard of defence in your favour, in the mighty name of Jesus Christ.

God will make you smile again over every issue that causes you trouble of mind and secret tears in the mighty name of Jesus Christ.

SECTION EIGHT (8):

Thank God for not allowing perpetual civil war to exist in many parts of our country

Thank God for what He has done for you and every individual in churches. Ps 138

Let us bless the name of our Lord Jesus Christ for the growth of Christianity in all the Continent.

Prophetic Declarations

In the book of Numbers 22 and 23, it was recorded that King Balak hired Prophet Balaam to curse the children of Israel but instead of cursing them he blessed them, he said, "How can I curse whom God had blessed?"

Therefore, I stand upon the Holy word of God and I speak to your Life and Destiny, because you have been blessed of the Lord.

Everyone that has been hired and paid to curse you, and your loved ones, the Almighty God will take over their mouth and begin to bless you.

The Almighty God will handover to you all the good fortunes of the world.

Everyone waiting to see you cry will surely come together to celebrate with you in Jesus' name.

SECTION NINE (9):

Thank God for mercy on the family of our spiritual leaders.

Thank God for divine health in the family of our spiritual leaders

Bless the name of the Lord for backing our spiritual leaders up in the ministry

Prophetic Declarations

Dream Killers, Vision Arresters and Opportunity Wasters, will be far from your life this year, their weapons will not prosper against your life and family, in the name of Jesus.

In this year of MANIFESTATION OF EXPECTATIONS (Romans 8:19, Proverbs 23:18), the songs of victory you could not sing last year shall become popular this year, in the name of Jesus. Psalm 89:20-29, Isaiah 54:13-17.

SECTION TEN (10):

Thank God for providing for our home.

Bless the name of the Lord for His mercies over our home.

Take your personal prayer points.

Thank you Lord for answered prayers.

Sing songs of praise and thanksgiving; thanking God in advance for answered prayers.

Keep serving God faithfully and trusting Him as you wait patiently for your harvest of testimonies! (Exodus 23:25)

Prophetic Declarations

If the Son therefore shall make you free, ye shall be free indeed. (John 8:36)

every evil invisible rope and satanic chain that has been used to tie your life and destiny down to a spot by the power of darkness shall be cut into pieces and burnt into ashes so that you can gain your liberty at last, in the mighty name of Jesus Christ.

God will hold you by the hands to walk you through great open doors of undeniable business and career opportunities, in the mighty name of Jesus Christ.

SECTION ELEVEN (11):

Thank you Father for what you are going to do in my life this year. Isaiah 43:19

Thank you Father for my glorious future. Psalm 67:5-7

Thank you Father for your manifestation in my life.

Prophetic Declarations

Let me pass through thy land: I will go along by the high way, I will neither turn unto the right hand nor to the left (Deuteronomy 2:27)

Wherever you have taken two steps forward and ten steps backward in any area of your life, the spirit of God will empower you and strengthen your steps to keep moving forward without looking backward anymore, in the mighty name of Jesus Christ.

There shall be no hiding places for the wicked in your family affairs, business and vocation in the mighty name of Jesus Christ.

SECTION TWELVE (12):

Thank God for His awesome moves in our church. Ps 136

Thank God for our spiritual leaders and for His mercy on them Exod. 33:19.

Thank God for calling and backing up our spiritual leaders in the ministry.

Prophetic Declarations

Blotting out the handwriting of ordinances that was against us, which was contrary to us, and took it out of the way, nailing it to his cross; (Colossians 2:14)

As you enter into this mid-week, any mark of failure, lack, delay, setback and no achievements noticeable upon any area of your life shall be blotted out by the blood of Jesus Christ.

Angels of God will offer you help in place of weakness in your life, in the mighty name of Jesus Christ.

SECTION THIRTEEN (13):

Thank God for not allowing the enemy to have none of his ways on our church Ps. 124.

Thank God for being our help in ages past. Ps. 121:1-8

Thank God for this year and for all the promises of God that are in it.

Prophetic Declarations

And Samuel said unto Jesse, Are here all thy children? And he said, There remaineth yet the youngest, and, behold, he keepeth the sheep. And Samuel said unto Jesse, Send and fetch him: for we will not sit down till he come hither (1 Samuel 16:11)

As the Lord God of heaven lives, every satanic majority vote cast against the will of God for your life, shall be cancelled and rendered null and void, in the mighty name of Jesus.

Every evil fire burning in your life shall be quenched and put out by the water of the Holy Spirit, in the mighty name of Jesus.

SECTION FOURTEEN (14):

Thank God for all the souls won through our spiritual leaders' ministry

Thank God for not allowing the enemy to cage us and our home.

I thank you for you will fill my mouth with praise and laughter this year in Jesus name.

Prophetic Declarations

And the LORD discomfited them before Israel, and slew them with a great slaughter at Gibeon, and chased them along the way that goeth up to Bethhoron, and smote them to Azekah, and unto Makkedah (Joshua 10:10)

Every evil meeting, organized to hold, as against the will of God for your life, shall be scattered by the mighty hands of the Lord operating against the conveners, in the wonderful name of Jesus.

As the Lord God of heaven lives, whatever could not allow the voice of your fore fathers to be heard in relevant high places, shall never have dominion over your own case. Now your voice shall be heard in relevant high places in life, in the mighty name of Jesus.

SECTION FIFTEEN (15):

Thank God for what He has done for you and every individual life. Ps 138

Thank God on behalf of the Church

Thank Him for all the prophecies being fulfilled and prayers already answered.

Prophetic Declarations

And by a prophet the LORD brought Israel out of Egypt, and by a prophet was he preserved.

(Hosea 12:13)

Just as God used Barnabas for Saul to achieve recognition before the church elders in Jerusalem, the same way, God will use human agents for you to penetrate into your promised land in business and career, in the mighty name of Jesus.

Judas hanged himself by reason of self condemnation, the same way every evil perpetrator around your life shall be made to commit suicide so that you can enjoy your life, in the mighty name of Jesus.

SECTION SIXTEEN (16):

Lord I bless you for all the signs and wonders you performed my life and family in previous year.

Lord I thank you for how you have started with me and your church this year

Thank Him for His ever-increasing anointing over our life and upon the rest of the family.

Prophetic Declarations

Moreover I will appoint a place for my people Israel, and will plant them, that they may dwell in a place of their own, and move no more; neither shall the children of wickedness afflict them any more, as beforetime, (2 Samuel 7:10)

Every repeated cycle of losses in your life shall be converted to unstoppable success galore, in the mighty name of Jesus.

God will command his light to shine out of every form of darkness existing in your life, in the mighty name of Jesus.

SECTION SEVENTEEN (17):

Thank you Lord for preserving the lives of my children

Thanks you Father for the new move in raising a new army of vibrant youths in our church Isa. 43:18-19

Prophetic Declarations

Saying, Where is he that is born King of the Jews? for we have seen his star in the east, and are come to worship him (Matthew 2:2)

As the day breaks this morning, your star shall be noticed in high places and shall continue to shine unto perfection, in the mighty name of Jesus.

Evils in your father's and your mother's house shall never catch up with your destiny, in the mighty name of Jesus.

SECTION EIGHTEEN (18):

1. Thank you Father for sending your son, Jesus, to set me free...

Thank you Father for the salvation of my soul and for all that you have endowed me with.

Prophetic Declarations

And I will restore to you the years that the locust hath eaten, the cankerworm, and the caterpiller, and the palmerworm, my great army which I sent among you (Joel 2:25)

Everything the devil and his agents negotiated for in your life by reason of your ignorance shall be commanded to be restored back to you with immediate effects, in the mighty name of Jesus.

Whenever the wicked ones mark out your life and possession for attacks, the blood of Jesus will cancel out their evil marks in the mighty name of Jesus.

SECTION NINETEEN (19):

Holy Spirit I thank you for you are always there for me.

Father, I praise you for all the testimonies (you can mention the testimonies) you have given me in year

Lord that rule in the affairs of men, I give you all glory for you have the power to do all things

Jesus I thank you for your provisions and the work of my hands

Prophetic Declarations

And fear came on all that dwelt round about them: and all these sayings were noised abroad throughout all the hill country of Judaea (Luke 1:65)

In whatever capacity your popularity has been reduced by the antics of men, the integrity of the lord will spread your fame abroad in the mighty name of Jesus.

Wherever circumstances of life have defeated you in time past, the Almighty God will lift up your hands there in total victory, in the mighty name of Jesus.

SECTION TWENTY (20):

FATHER, I THANK YOU

Psalm 95:1-7 & Psalm 96:1-13

Lord be thou exalted above all the earth, heavens and other gods.

Jesus I thank you for the gift of life that you have given me and my family.

All glory, honour and power be unto Jesus who has not allowed my enemies to rejoice over me

I thank you Jesus for you'll make me conquered year.

Father, I thank you for this great year of abundant blessings for me and my household

Prophetic Declarations

And a river went out of Eden to water the garden; and from thence it was parted, and became into four heads (Genesis 2:10)

God will rain down his showers of blessings upon you today, and every dryness affecting your operations in life shall be converted to a watered garden, in the mighty name of Jesus.

God of heaven will respond to your need for help early enough in your life, in the mighty name of Jesus.

SECTION TWENTY-ONE (21):

UNUSUAL APPRECIATION

Thank God for His awesome moves. Ps 136

Thank God for His provision in all your ways.

Thank God for not allowing the enemies to have of their ways

Thank God for the family and for His mercy on them Exod. 33:19

Prophetic Declarations

Exodus 3:21-"And I will give this people favour in the sight of the Egyptians; and it shall be, when you go, that you shall not go empty-handed".

As you go out this year, you will not return home empty-handed.

The Lord shall load you with abundant blessings just as the Egyptians loaded God's people with various gifts when they were leaving Egypt.

You will not crossover with afflictions, debts and unhappiness.

All your outstanding blessings from January shall be packaged for you before the end of the year in Jesus mighty Name.

SECOND DIVISION: ASKING FOR DIVINE MERCY

SECTION ONE (1):

DIVINE MERCY

What is the Divine Mercy?

Divine Mercy is to Trust in God's unconditional Love and Mercy and practice merciful love to our neighbour in deed, word and prayer.

This shows the relationship between the concept of Love and the concept of Mercy, revealing the true meaning of selfless Love manifested as Mercy.

The Divine Mercy message is one we can call to mind simply by remembering ABC:

A - Ask for His Mercy. God wants us to approach Him in prayer constantly, repenting of our sins and asking Him to pour His mercy out upon us and upon the whole world.

B - Be merciful. God wants us to receive His mercy and let it flow through us to others. He wants us to extend love and forgiveness to others just as He does to us.

C - Completely trust in Jesus. God wants us to know that the graces of His mercy are dependent upon our trust. The more we trust in Jesus, the more we will receive.

Spend time to learn more about the mercy of God, learn to trust in Jesus, and live your life as merciful to others, as Christ is merciful to you.

The Lord wants us to do these works of mercy, because even the strongest faith is of no use without works.

Corporal Works

- Feed the hungry
- Give drink to the thirsty
- Clothe the naked
- Shelter the homeless
- Visit the prisoners
- Comfort the sick
- Bury the dead

Spiritual Works

- Teach the ignorant
- Pray for the living and dead
- Correct sinners
- Counsel those in doubt
- Console the sorrowful
- Bear wrongs patiently
- Forgive wrongs willingly

What are the Works of Mercy?

Let your Mercy be in Action

Jesus said, "Blessed are the merciful, for they shall obtain mercy" (Matthew 5:7).

PRAYERS

Father, we appreciate You for a bright new day, week and month; to You be all the glory Lord in Jesus' Name (Ps. 92:1-2)

Father, I access Your Presence today by the Blood of Jesus in the Name of Jesus (Heb. 10:19)

Father, I ask for the establishment of Your rule, reign, will and plan for this week, for my life, for this Commission and this Nation in Jesus' Name (Matt. 6:9-10)

By the Lord's mercies I cannot be consumed!

Father, I come before You today and apply for fresh mercy for my life, family and loved ones; I cannot be destroyed or wasted this week in Jesus' Name'; by Your mercy, nobody connected, associated or related with me can be destroyed this week or beyond in Jesus' Name

Father, by Your mercy, I receive a productive, successful and impactful week; I shall experience a fruitful week and not a wasted week in Jesus' Name

Father, visit me, like You visited Moses, Gideon and Saul; in this season of Divine visitation and manifestation, I receive a visitation NOW!

Father, as we go out as a Church to seek the lost, help us to see Your unbelievable and unusual acts; this week, we make demands for a harvest of souls in Jesus' Name! (Mark 16:20)

I receive a baptism of the Spirit of Wisdom NOW!

Talk to God about anything you want Him to do for you this week

Thank You Lord for answered prayers

Prophetic Declarations

1 Chronicles 4:10 And Jabez called on the God of Israel, saying, Oh that thou wouldest bless me indeed, and enlarge my coast, and

that thine hand might be with me, and that thou wouldest keep me from evil, that it may not grieve me! And God granted him that which he requested.

By the mercies of the almighty God, the lord will exceedingly enlarge your coast this year. God will give you additional multiple sources of income in Jesus mighty name.

- What is yours must enter your hands!

- This week must be productive, successful and impactful; your results this week shall be greater than all your results of this year so far!

- What the devil is planning shall never come to pass!

- There shall be no accident, loss, calamity or tragedy!

SECTION TWO (2):

FATHER LET ME EXPERIENCE THE POWER OF MERCY.

2 kings 25:27-30.2 Samuel 9:1-13.Hoseah 14:4-7.Jeremiah 30:16-18.Isaiah 14:1-3.

What is Mercy?

Mercy is kindness, Forbear to harm, Uncountable forgiveness, Compassion especially to the less fortunate, tender-heartedness, Empathy, Pity.

Associate of mercy: Love, Remembrance, Promotion, New beginning, Not by merit but mercy

Examples

Mephibosheth,

Jehoiachin

“So then it is not of him that willeth, nor of him that runneth but of God that sheweth mercy” (Roman 9:16)

Divine grace gets things done quicker. It is not based on merit and not dependent on your past but an unmerited favour of God bequeathed on a person. Grace makes you blessed even when you do not look like it. It increases you beyond your efforts. If you ever made anything happen, it is because of grace; for nothing terminates disgrace like grace.

Know that every successful story is a product of labour. Hard work will amount to nothing without grace. You will not be disgraced. 2 Kings 25:27-30. 2 Samuel 9:1-13.

Prayer of Repentance, Mercy And Grace

Let the wicked forsake his way, and the unrighteous man his thoughts; let him return to the Lord, that he may have compassion on him, and to our God, for he will abundantly pardon. (Isaiah 55:7)

Sing quality praise and worship songs to the Almighty God.

1. Confess your sins, ask for forgiveness and cleansing by the blood of Jesus.

2. Father, I confess the sins of my ancestors and family including cheating, adultery,

fornication, stealing, prostitution, slavery, drunkenness, etc.

3. I ask for pardon and forgiveness in Jesus name.

4. Father, let the blood of Jesus cleanse me from all my sins in Jesus name.

5. Holy Ghost fire, consume the root of sin from my life in Jesus mighty name.

6. Ancestral sins will not destroy my future in Jesus name.

7. Lord, deliver me from presumptuous sins, thoughts and acts that I do not know are sinful

in Jesus name.

8. I confess and repent of every sin I have committed knowingly or unknowingly.

9. Father, let the blood of Jesus wash away every sin, spot, blemish and uncleanness in my

life.

10. Father, let the blood of Jesus wash away the effects of every ancestral sin in Jesus name.

11. Father, let your mercy remove every hindrance resulting from sins in Jesus name.

12. Father, give me the grace to take steps to correct misdeeds that should be corrected in Jesus

name.

13. Sin will not hinder my shining in Jesus name.

14. I will not lack, I will have more than enough in Jesus name.

15. Thank you Lord for answered prayers.

Prophetic Declarations

And the LORD spake unto the fish, and it vomited out Jonah upon the dry land (Jonah 2:10)

This morning, upon your every satanic "big fish" that has swallowed the glory of God upon your life shall speedily vomit it up again in order to let you go free into your destiny, in the mighty name of Jesus.

And every evil manipulation that has wrapped round your breakthroughs shall be punctured and terminated to set you free in the mighty name of Jesus.

SECTION THREE (3):

MERCY FOR YOUR SAKE

1 KINGS 15:2-5

"Nevertheless for David's sake did the Lord his God give him a lamp in Jerusalem, to set up his son after him, and to establish Jerusalem" (1 Kings 15:4).

THIS IS MY SEASONS OF MERCY

In our text, it was only for David's sake that God spared Abijam, his great grandson. Be right with God and be holy. God can show mercy and bless your family just for your sake.

PRAYER

Lord, please make me a blessing to my family, neighbours and friends.

Let every counsel of the wicked against me be frustrated in Jesus name.

Let every power challenging my advancement and greatness, die in Jesus name (Ephesians 6: 10-12, Isaiah 9:5).

I will prevail over every opposition in Jesus name.

I will not miss my crowning and celebration hour in Jesus name.

I recover every good thing I have lost as a result of sins in Jesus name.

Lord, restore to me the joy of your salvation and give me your Holy Spirit.

I receive the grace and power of the Holy Spirit to live above sin in Jesus name.

Evil warders assigned against me to enforce satanic imprisonment upon my life, family, career, finances and destiny; die in the mighty name of Jesus (repeat three times).

Powers trying to dispossess me of my God-given blessings, power, authority and high places; die in the name of Jesus.

Powers that want me to exist as one who is dead while still living, die in the name of Jesus.

Powers that wants to dispossess me of my rightful authority, positioning and destiny, die in the name of Jesus.

Satanic plans against my rising, die in Jesus name.

Take your personal prayer points.

Thank you Lord for answered prayers.

Prophetic Declarations

He taketh the wise in their own craftiness: and the counsel of the froward is carried headlong. (Job 5:13)

As from this morning, if there is any secret agent of Satan operating around your life and destiny, tormenting and frustrating your efforts, God will expose them and disconnect their source of information and they shall no longer have dominion over your life again, in the mighty name of Jesus.

may the aroma of favour in Christ Jesus perfume your life with divine attractions for supernatural helps from people that matters in quarters higher than your level of operations in the natural, in the mighty name of Jesus.

SECTION FOUR (4):

ACCELERATED MERCY

"O satisfy us early with thy mercy; that we may rejoice and be glad all our days".

Psalm 90:12 KJV.

We all need urgent mercy from the Lord in these perilous times. The Almighty has to speedily intervene so the heathens can know that our Redeemer lives. If our blessings get delayed further than bearable, the enemies will say “Where is now thy God?” (Psalm 3.1-2,Psalm 38:22, Psalm 141:1)

God has made adequate provisions for us and is willing to satisfy our needs upon our requests from sincere hearts. “Thou shalt arise, and have mercy upon Zion: for the time to favour her, yea, the set time, is come." Psalms 102:13.

Examples:

1. Woman with issue of blood: Her miracle could no longer be delayed. She pushed her way through by faith.(Mark 5:25-29).

2. Hannah: Year in, year out, she went to Shiloh, until she cried her way to fruitfulness and God opened her womb (1 Samuel 1:26-28)

3. Centurion: His desperation made him declare "Master just speak the Word" (Matt.8:8-13)

4. YOU: Like Bartimaeus, cry out loud and clear: "Jesus Thou Son of David, have mercy on me."

What to do:

1. Place an urgent order or demand on your request to the Lord.

2. Never give up, ask until you get it.

3. Step out in faith and doubt not.

4. Praise God ahead of the blessings.

Prayer Points:

1. Father thank You for my day has come at last.

2. Father, satisfy me early with Your mercy; don't let age and time catch up on me.

3. Father, let me rejoice and be glad all my days.

4. Father, show Your mercy upon Your church, so the heathens can bow to Your great name.

5. Thank you Lord for answered prayers.

Prophetic Declarations

The steps of a goodman are ordered by the LORD: and he delighteth in his way.(Psalm 37:23)

as you wake up this morning and for the remaining days for this year to end

the lord will order your steps and direct your hands to make uncommon progress and do supernatural exploits in business and career, in the mighty name of Jesus Christ.

Every step you have miscalculated in time past shall be supernaturally reordered to achieve your desired purpose in life, in the mighty name of Jesus Christ.

SECTION FIVE (5):

MERCY OF JESUS, PURGE ME FROM THE MESS OF SIN

Sin is the reason for the erosion of dignity and destiny. Many have lost their dignity on the altar of iniquity in this world and in eternity. But Jesus Christ brought salvation in the place of condemnation; He brought mercy and purity in the place of mess and impurity; He brought life in the place of death. He brought grace to assist us to keep the Word of God.

“When Jesus had lifted up himself, and saw none but the woman, he said unto her, Woman, where are those thine accusers? hath no man condemned thee? She said, No man, Lord. And Jesus said unto her, Neither do I condemn thee: go, and sin no more." John 8:10-11

Our anchor Scripture tells a story of a woman who was caught in a terrible mess, the sin of adultery. The sin was so serious that it attracted death by stoning based on the Law of Moses. So, the woman was to be stoned to death. The Jews and the Scribes brought her to Jesus to ask if the law should be applied on her or not. And by so doing, they were also trying to trap Jesus so as to find something to use against Him.

But Jesus had compassion on the woman and saved her from being destroyed without giving the Jews any ground for accusing Him of breaking the Law of Moses. You see, but for the mercy of Jesus the woman would have perished in the mess of her sin.

Sin is the reason for the erosion of dignity and destiny. Many have lost their dignity on the altar of iniquity in this world and in eternity. But Jesus Christ brought salvation in the place of condemnation; He brought mercy and purity in the place of mess and impurity; He brought life in the place of death. He brought grace to assist us to keep the Word of God.

PRAYER

1. In the name of Jesus, my children shall not see evil any more. Zephaniah 3:15

2. Jesus of Nazareth, bless my children and make them blessings unto nations in the name of

Jesus. Genesis 22:18

3. Jesus, destroy anything that will make my children a grief of mind unto me and the Lord in

the name of Jesus. Genesis 28:41

4. Lord Jesus, let my children be glorified with thee in the name of Jesus. Romans 8:17

5. Lord, make my children good ambassadors for Christ in the name of Jesus. 2 Corinthians 5:20

6. From every evil yoke, I receive my freedom by God's mercy in Jesus name.

7. From every hard yoke of bondage in Jesus name, I receive my freedom, by the mercy of God

8. Periodic warfare from the pit of hell attacking my breakthrough by the mercy of God be

aborted in Jesus name.

9. Dream attacks swallowing my blessing, I command by God's mercy be cancelled in Jesus

name.

10. Thank you Lord for answered prayers.

PROPHETIC DECLARATIONS

… one thing I know, that, whereas I was blind, now I see. (John 9:25)

Today, the Lord will redirect the course of your life and destiny to fulfil his divine plan for your future to deliver the expected results, in the mighty name of Jesus Christ.

Every supporter of your enemies shall loose their advantage position, in the mighty name of Jesus Christ.

SECTION SIX (6):

O LORD HAVE MERCY ON MY CHILDREN

Phil.4:13; Rev. 13:10; Zeph.3:15-20; Ps.107:20.

"Verily I say unto you, whatsoever ye shall bind on earth shall be bound in heaven: and whatsoever ye shall loose on earth shall be loosed in heaven". Mathew 18:18

PRAYERS

1. The birthright of my children shall not be taken away from them in the name of Jesus. Gen. 25:31

2. My children shall not bear the effects of the sins of their ancestors, in the mighty name of Jesus. Gen. 9:22, 25

3. Father Lord, let the life of any power planning evil against my children be cut off now, in the name of Jesus. Proverbs 10:27
4. Lord Jesus, loose every band of wickedness from my children, to thy glory. Isaiah 58:6

5. Father Lord, raise the foundation of my children on Christ the Rock, in the name of Jesus. Isaiah 58:12

6. The sun of my children shall not go down; neither shall their moon withdraw itself in the name of Jesus. Isaiah 60:20
7. The Lord shall be the everlasting light of my children all their days in the name of Jesus. Isaiah 60:20
8. Father Lord, have mercy on my children and do not remove your covenant of peace from

them in the mighty name of Jesus. Isaiah 54:10
9. No hair on the head of my children shall perish in the name of Jesus. Luke 21:18

10.Jesus, open great and effectual doors of favour and prosperity for my children in the name of Jesus. I Corinthians 16:9

11.Thank you Lord for answered prayers.

PROPHETIC DECLARATIONS

But he answered and said, Every plant, which my heavenly Father hath not planted, shall be rooted up. (Matthew 15:13)

as you wake up this morning, every force against your life and your establishment shall be uprooted and destroyed, so that you can take your rightful place in life and destiny, in the mighty name of Jesus Christ.

no evil shall come near your dwellings and every satanic procedure targeted against your life shall be completely nullified by the spirit of the lord, in the mighty name of Jesus Christ.

SECTION SEVEN (7):

O LORD SHOW ME GREAT MERCY

Numbers 14v18; Psalm 57v10; Psalm 86v13; Psalm 103v11, 108v4; Eph. 2v4; Joshua 10v11–14; Judges 6 & 7; 2 Kings 4v1-7; Psalm 102v13; Roman 9v14–16; Acts 5v18–19

CONFESSION

Psalm 86 v 13 – For great is thy mercy toward me: and thou hast delivered my soul from the lowest hell.

Mercy is a gift from God. It is underserved. If it were not for God's mercy, we all would have faced terrible judgments long ago. If not for His mercy, He would have condemned us after our first offence. If not for His mercy, He would punish us each time we sin, but rather than letting us bear the full punishment for our sin, God demonstrated His mercy when He paid the penalty for our sin Himself.

Psalm 6v2a – "Have mercy upon me O! Lord, for I am weak" is the heart felt cry of many.

PRAYERS

Mercy of God lift me up in Jesus name.

Lamentation 3 v 17 – any evil word from the mouth of men against my life, mercy of God, cancel them in Jesus name.

At the junction of confusion, mercy of God, bail me out in Jesus name.

From every ocean of failure, mercy of God, bail me out in Jesus name.

Lord, show me great mercy in Jesus name.

Great mercy of God, locate me in Jesus name.

PROPHETIC DECLARATIONS

Thou didst walk through the sea with thine horses, through the heap of great waters (Hab 3:15) this morning, into your life the impossible shall become cheaply possible for you in your family, in your vocation, in your business and in your career, in the mighty name of Jesus Christ.

the God of all round possibilities will align with you to do for you what others consider as impossibilities, in the mighty name of Jesus Christ.

SECTION EIGHT (8):

WHAT TRIGGERS GOD'S GREAT MERCY

Blind Bartemaeus asked for mercy before asking for his eyes to be opened, Mark 10v46–52. A prayer of desperation must be preceded by a cry for mercy. As you call on God, His great mercy shall locate you in Jesus name.

Be born-again - John 3 v 3

Get sanctified and filled with the Holy Ghost – Acts 1 v 4 – 5

Live a life of holiness - 1 Peter 1 v 15

Live a life of total obedience – Deut. 28 v 1, Isaiah 1 v 1 – 19

Live a life of absolute surrender and total yield – Galatians 2 v 20

Be kingdom-minded always – 1 Peter 4 v 7

Give faithfully – i.e. tithes, first fruits, kingdom project, seed etc.

Intercede for others, be a burden bearer – Luke 6 v 38

Remember the widows, orphans and the less privileged

Don't be logical with God and interfere with the laws and principles of God. Malachi 3 v 8 – 12. The foolishness of God is wiser than men, always remember 1 Cor. 1 v 25

Shun a sinful lifestyle - Jer. 5 v 25

Avoid bitterness, wrath, anger, clamour, malice, envy etc. Eph. 4 v 26 – 31

Be diligent in your work - Heb. 6 v 12, Proverbs 18 v 9 – God will not remember a lazy person.

Don't go to Egypt for help, depend on the Lord absolutely – Prov. 16 v 2 & 3; Isaiah 31 v 1 & 2

Let the fear of God rule your life – Prov. 19 v 23

Learn to give thanks always – 1 Thess 5 v 18

PRAYER:

By the great mercy of God, O Lord, restore my departed glory in Jesus name.

By the great mercy of God, all my captured blessings, be released in Jesus name.

By the great mercy of God, my positive dreams, manifest in Jesus name.

By the great mercy of God, I shall see no evil in my home in Jesus name.

By the great mercy of God, O Lord, deliver me from evil burdens in Jesus name.

By the great mercy of God, all my pending breakthroughs, manifest in Jesus name.

By the great mercy of God, all my benefits in chains, be loosed in Jesus name.

PROPHETIC DECLARATIONS

They that dwell under his shadow shall return; they shall revive as the corn, and grow as the vine: the scent thereof shall bear the wine of Lebanon. (Hosea 14:7)

This morning, in any area of your life where you have taken two steps forward and ten steps backward in time past, angels of god will partner with you to start moving forward with speed without looking backwards again, for ever and ever, in the mighty name of Jesus Christ.

God of heaven will watch over you to go forth and return peacefully in every journey you embark upon, in the mighty name of Jesus Christ.

SECTION NINE (9):

YOU NEED THE GREAT MERCY OF GOD NOW

When Did You Need It?

When you are in a complete mess

When it seems your vision is bigger than you.

When you are below the ground level on any matter.

When you are an executive beggar.(Educated but begging to survive)

When you have been totally condemned in the court of man, in fact they have said nothing good will come out of your Nazareth.

When all hope seems lost and you feel like giving up.

When no man can answer your questions.

When you are frustrated beyond description, in fact you cannot describe it. Your frustration is killing, shocking, stifling, chocking, unexplainable, embarrassing, and messy and even challenging your salvation.

When you are swimming in the ocean of failure and embarrassment

When men lied against you and no one believes you.

When you get demoted, instead of being promoted.

When everything around you fails.

When you are to meet an important deadline and your strength is failing. i.e. deadline panic.

When it seems age is no longer on your side.

When it seems eyes are not on you anymore i.e. people don't fancy you anymore.

When all your age mates have achieved and you are still behind.

When people are saying nothing good can happen to you.

When you are desperate to take a foolish step because of frustration.

When you have been written off by friends, family members and close allies.

When you feel no helper can locate you.

PRAYER

By the great mercy of God, doors of opportunities, be opened unto me in Jesus name.

By the great mercy of God, my book of remembrance, be opened in Jesus name.

By the great mercy of God, O Lord raise me up to the next level in Jesus name.

By the great mercy of God, all anti-progress altars erected against me, scatter in Jesus name.

By the great mercy of God, my life/destiny, be withdrawn from any evil control in Jesus name.

By the great mercy of God, anointing of the overcomer, fall on me in Jesus name.

By the great mercy of God, anointing to possess my possessions fall on me in Jesus name.

It is my prayer that the great mercy of the Almighty God will bring something good out of you, and bring out your testimonies in Jesus name.

PROPHETIC DECLARATIONS

Hast not thou made an hedge about him, and about his house, and about all that he hath on every side? thou hast blessed the work of his hands, and his substance is increased in the land. (Job 1:10)

Today, the lord will make an everlasting hedge of protection and supernatural preservation about your family and all your possessions, in the mighty name of Jesus Christ.

May the Lord bless the work of your hands and preserve it at the same time against every act of wickedness, in the mighty name of Jesus Christ.

SECTION TEN (10):

SOME HINDERANCES TO GOD'S GREAT MERCY

2 Cor. 6 v 14 – 16

Deliberate sin, Keeping accursed/demonic materials, Using false measures, Engaging in illegal businesses, Taking bribe/graft, Unforgiveness, malice, wrath, envy etc.

PRAYER

Lord, show me the broken walls You want me to rebuild.

Use me to rebuild the broken foundations in my life and in the lives of others. I pray in Jesus name.

From every ocean of failure, mercy of God, bail me out in Jesus name.

Lord, show me great mercy in Jesus name.

From every form of negative attitude, mercy of God bail me out.

From the spirit of fear, mercy of God, bail me out.

From laziness in prayers, mercy of God, bail me out.

From laziness in studying the word of God, bail me out.

From lack of watchfulness, mercy of God, bail me out.

From procrastination, mercy of God, bail me out.

PROPHETIC DECLARATIONS

Who art thou that judgest another man's servant? to his own master he standeth or falleth. Yea, he shall be holden up: for God is able to make him stand. (Rom 14:4)

This morning, every satanic and unfair judge, taking side with your accusers to torment and create pains for you, shall be condemned and judged for your sake, in the mighty name of Jesus Christ.

The lord will uphold you and make you stand in every area of your weakness, in the mighty name of Jesus Christ.

SECTION ELEVEN (11)

BIBLICAL CASES OF THOSE THAT ENJOYED THE GREAT MERCY OF GOD

Elizabeth – her neighbour and cousins heard of the great mercy shown to her and they rejoiced with her. Luke 1 v 57 - 58

Joseph was shown mercy that MADE him in life. He became notable in life by the great mercy of God. Gen. 39 v 21

Solomon reiterated the fact that God showed David his father great mercy, by making him have a son on the throne in Israel. 2 Chronicles 1 v 8

Daughter of Abraham - Luke 13 v 11 – 17

The man born blind - John 9 v 1 – 7

Jeremiah regained his freedom – Jeremiah 40 v 1 – 4

Daniel in the lion's den - Daniel 6 v 16 – 23

The Shunamite Woman, gift of a son, and the raising afterwards of the son from the dead. 2 Kings 4 v 14 – 37

PRAYER

Great mercy of God, locate me in Jesus name.

By the great mercy of God, my book of remembrance, be opened in Jesus name.

By the great mercy of God, all anti-progress altars erected against me, scatter in Jesus name.

By the great mercy of God, my life/destiny, be withdrawn from any evil control in Jesus name.

By the great mercy of God, anointing of the overcomer, fall on me in Jesus name.

By the great mercy of God, anointing to possess my possessions fall on me in Jesus name.

From every hard yoke of bondage in Jesus name, I receive my freedom, by the mercy of God.

Periodic warfare from the pit of hell attacking my breakthrough by the mercy of God be aborted in Jesus name.

Dream attacks swallowing my blessing, I command by God's mercy, be cancelled in Jesus name.

PROPHETIC DECLARATIONS

And he dreamed yet another dream, and told it his brethren, and said, Behold, I have dreamed a dream more; and, behold, the sun and the moon and the eleven stars made obeisance to me. (Genesis 37:9)

This morning, it is my earnest and heartfelt prayers for you that your spiritual eyes may be opened to see the revelation of every hidden greatness in you in order to be empowered for it's fulfillment, in the mighty name of Jesus Christ.

may your talent and gift connect you with people that matters in announcing your greatness in your field of relevance in life, in the mighty name of Jesus Christ.

SECTION TWO (12):

WHAT DOES GOD'S MERCY DO FOR YOU?

1. God's mercy turns a rejected person into the accepted and beloved.

2. God's mercy levels insurmountable obstacles turning them into stepping stones for greatness.

3. God's mercy turns a nonentity into the cornerstone of a family or community.

4. That God will have mercy on whom He chooses to have mercy. Exodus 33:19.

5. The mercy of God is God's kindness in action. Psalm 51:1.

6. God's mercy secures our pardon from the wages of sin which is death. Romans 6:23, 1 Corinthians 15:10, Ephesians 2:4-5.

7. Mercy obtains for us help at the time of need. Hebrews 4:15-17.

8. Mercy is not dependent on our ability or strength but God's grace. Romans 9:16.

9. Mercy is not earned but granted by God's grace alone. Hebrews 4:16.

PRAYER

1. Mercy of God, lift me up in Jesus name.

2. Lamentation 3 vs 17 – any evil word from the mouth of men against my life, mercy of God, cancel them in Jesus name.

3. At the junction of confusion, mercy of God, bail me out in Jesus name.

4. Father, let every broken wall of my life be mended in the name of Jesus.

5. Father, let every financial broken wall of my life be mended in the name of Jesus name.

6. Father, let every broken wall in my family be mended in the name of Jesus.

7. Father, let every broken wall in my career be mended in the name of Jesus name.

8. Father, let every broken wall in my work be mended in the name of Jesus name.

9. Father, help us to mend every broken wall in the house of God in the name of Jesus.

PROPHETIC DECLARATIONS

From henceforth let no man trouble me: for I bear in my body the marks of the Lord Jesus. (Gal 6:17)

this morning, may the marks of Christ upon your life become visible for the enemies to see, so as not to be able to come near you for affliction or manipulations again, in the mighty name of Jesus Christ.

The marks of Christ you bear upon your body will definitely put an end to every affliction of your glorious life and destiny, in the mighty name of Jesus Christ.

SECTION THREE (13):

LORD, PLEASE HAVE MERCY ON OUR LAND.

"If my people, which are called by my name, shall humble themselves, and pray, and seek my face, and turn from their wicked ways; then will I hear from heaven, and will forgive their sin, and will heal their land." 2 Chronicles□ 7:14□ KJV□□.□□□□□□□□

It is time to earnestly call on the Lord God ,for mercy for the country with the largest population of blacks in the world.Every Nation or Kingdom on earth at some points in history, will go through very serious period of hardship. The response of the ruler ship and the people to God's principles always determine which way the pendulum swings.

PRAYER:

1. Father, thank You for NIGERIA, the land of our birth, please forgive all our sins.

2. Father, we humble ourselves and ask for complete, cleansing and restoration of our Land.

3. Father, we repent of all our evil ways, from the leadership and follower-ship, from the pulpit

to the pews, from the learned to the ignorant.

4. Father, please create in us new and sincere patriotic hearts, ready to obey Your will totally.

5. Father, we have suffered enough as a Nation, please start afresh with us with Your love

mercy and salvation.

6. Father let NIGERIA take her rightful position in the comity of Nations and make us highly

productive again.

7. Father let our land become indeed the nation of the Lord and a good example to the whole world.

PROPHETIC DECLARATIONS

So shall the king greatly desire thy beauty: for he is thy Lord; and worship thou him. (Psalm 45:11)

I pray for you today in the name that is above all other names, that men and women of great worth and dignity shall see and honour the name of Jesus Christ in your life. That name will take away your reproach and shame of many years and by that name all your steps in life shall be accorded with great favours, in the mighty name of Jesus Christ.

Every household and domestic problem, disturbing and destabilizing your progress in life, shall be uprooted today, in the mighty name of Jesus Christ.

SECTION FOUR (14):

KEYS TO UNLOCK DIVINE MERCY

Matthew 5:7-"Blessed are the merciful: for they shall obtain mercy."_

One of the greatest jackpots you can ever win is to qualify for the mercies of God!

How much of divine mercy you can access from God will determine how glorious your life will be per time and over time-_"And that he might make known the riches of his glory on the vessels of mercy, which he had afore prepared unto glory"_ Rom. 9:23

But to be an undeniable candidate of divine mercy, you must be addicted to showing mercy to others- _"With the merciful thou wilt shew thyself merciful, and with the upright man thou wilt shew thyself upright."_ 2Sam.22:26

When you show mercy unto others, God will have no option but to shower you will His mercies! The only one that can miss divine mercy is anyone that believes that he is wiser than God.

PRAYER

O Lord make me addicted to showing mercy unto others so as to enjoy your showers of mercies and blessings on earth and in eternity in Jesus name._

PROPHETIC DECLARATIONS

Wherefore they cried unto the LORD, and said, We beseech thee, O LORD, we beseech thee, let us not perish for this man's life, and lay not upon us innocent blood: for thou, O LORD, hast done as it pleased thee.(Jonah 1:14)

I assure you of this one thing that the God of heaven will surely fight for you, protect you, rescue you from destructions and he will not allow your blood to be spilled on the highways in the journeys of your life, in the mighty name of Jesus Christ.

This is what will happen from today; every network of the devil with which the enemies are monitoring your life shall be permanently disabled, in the mighty name of Jesus Christ.

SECTION FIVE (15):

WHO NEEDS THIS MERCYAND WHAT DOES GOD'S MERCY DO FOR YOU?

Today's prayer is for you if you are currently facing challenges, doubts, rejection, neglect, fears and phobias, despise, struggles, downturns, bad-luck, insecurities, other negative things. It is for:

1. It is for anyone who is looking up to God for upliftment.

2. It is for anyone here who is going through a wilderness experience and wondering if He will ever get out of it.

3. It is for anyone that is feeling despondent and as if he or she has reached the end of the road.

PRAYER

By the great mercy of God, O Lord, restore my departed glory in Jesus name.

By the great mercy of God, all my captured blessings, be released in Jesus name.

By the great mercy of God, my positive dreams, manifest in Jesus name.

By the great mercy of God, O Lord, deliver me from evil burdens in Jesus name.

By the great mercy of God, all my pending breakthroughs, manifest in Jesus name.

By the great mercy of God, all my benefits in chains be loosed in Jesus name.

PROPHETIC DECLARATIONS

O send out thy light and thy truth: let them lead me; let them bring me unto thy holy hill, and to thy tabernacles. (Psalm 43:3)

May the ray of supernatural sunlight reveal your inner treasures to your benefactors and empower your mind to receive it's attendant blessings, in the mighty name of Jesus Christ.

May the power of supernatural establishment confirm your dominion and authority over every work of the enemies in your life, in the mighty name of Jesus Christ.

SECTION SIX (16):

PRAYER

From carelessness, mercy of God, bail me out.

From treating God's word/instruction with levity, mercy of God, bail me out.

By the great mercy of God, doors of opportunities, be opened unto me in Jesus name.

From every evil yoke, I receive my freedom by God's mercy in Jesus name.

O! Lord my father, I surrender this situation (mention it) unto you, take over from me.

My ordained great achievement manifest in Jesus name.

My great achievement in any captivity, rebel, jump out and locate me in Jesus name.

This is my year of great achievement; I shall achieve and manifest greatness throughout this year in Jesus name.

My foundation will not sink my great achievement in Jesus name.

I shall manifest great achievement in all areas of my life this year in Jesus name.

PROPHETIC DECLARATIONS

"Surely goodness and mercy shall follow me all the days of my life: and I will dwell in the house of the LORD for ever" (Psalm 23:6)

as you wake up this morning, i decree by the decree of heaven, i decree the unity of all covenant forces of advancement and breakthroughs to work in your favour, in the mighty name of Jesus Christ and every stranger fuelling crisis and sponsoring afflictions in your life shall be brought down to powerlessness by the authority of heaven, in the mighty name of Jesus Christ.

SECTION SEVEN (17):

"So the people shouted when the priests blew the trumpets: and it came to pass, when the people heard the sound of the trumpet, and the people shouted with a great shout, that the wall fell down flat, so that the people went up into the city, every man straight before him, and they took the city" (Joshua 6:20)

today, the invisible angels of god will destroy every satanic wall of partition between you and your benefactor and your inheritance, in the mighty name of Jesus Christ.

major events of your life that the enemies have suspended over a period of time shall be speedily visited for quick action, in the mighty name of Jesus Christ.

PRAYER

O Lord my Father have mercy on me.

Jesus Son of David have mercy on me and forgive me all my sins.

Jesus Son of David have mercy on me and move my life forward.

Mercy of God arise and make room for me, in the name of Jesus.

O God arise by your mercy and keep and preserve my life.

By the mercy of God, I declare that this is my year of joy in the name of Jesus.

O Lord remember me always because of your great mercies.

O Lord, by your mercy, uproot everything in my life that you have not planted.

By your great mercy Lord, break all bondages that are harassing my life.

By your great mercies Lord, let the wickedness of the wicked upon my life be turned upon their own heads.

Jesus by your great mercies, honor and glory shall not be scarce in my life, in the name of Jesus.

I shall see and experience the mercy of God in all areas of my life, in the name of Jesus.

PROPHETIC DECLARATIONS

But we all, with open face beholding as in a glass the glory of the Lord, are changed into the same image from glory to glory, even as by the Spirit of the Lord. (2 Corinthians 3:18)

as you appear before the Lord in Zion this morning, the God of heaven will impart your efforts in life with enviable glory and success that will turn things around in your favour, in the mighty name of Jesus Christ.

God of heaven will refashion your life and destiny to fulfill his original plan for your generation, in the mighty name of Jesus Christ.

SECTION EIGHT (18):

FATHER LET ME BENEFIT GOD'S MERCY

God's mercy purges our sins and iniquities. Proverbs 3:1-4.

God's mercy brings favor with men and with God. Genesis 39:21.

Victory over unfavorable circumstances and men. Psalm 59:10, 136:24.

God' faithfulness and preservation. Job 10:12.

Opens the heavens over a person's life so that prayers are answered and blessings abound. Luke 1:30-32.

Affords new beginnings and new things. Psalm 32:10.

Brings honor and glory. Psalm 89:24.

Keeps you from falling. Genesis 6:9.

Restoration. Joel 2:25.

PRAYER

I decree and declare that darkness will not overshadow my great achievement throughout this year and beyond in Jesus name.

My ordained great achievement for this year shall not be padlocked in Jesus name.

My great scheduled for this year, reject delay, calamities, drowning, downfall in Jesus name.

I decree, that any great achievement shall attract wealth/riches and prosperity in Jesus name.

By the help and mercies of God, this year I shall enlarge, break forth, expand, and cover new grounds in Jesus name.

Blood of Jesus, cover my life and family in the name of Jesus.

Every evil attempt to terminate my life and family this year, be aborted in the name of Jesus.

Evil attempt to enslave my glory this year or in future by any dark agent, be aborted in the name of Jesus.

Any attempt to fire arrows of mistake and error into my life, work, family or marriage, be destroyed by fire in Jesus name.

Every evil attempt to stop my progress, now or in future, fail woefully in Jesus name.

PROPHETIC DECLARATIONS

Then said the LORD unto me, Thou hast well seen: for I will hasten my word to perform it (Jeremiah 1:12)

This morning, the vision you have for your life shall receive divine backing with speedy supernatural accomplishments in all areas, in the mighty name of Jesus Christ.

SECTION NINETEEN (19):

TO WHOM DOES GOD SHOW HIS MERCY?

God showers His mercy on the following groups of people:

1. Those that know Him and have become His friends. Proverbs 3:1-4.
2. Those that obey His word and keep His commandments. Psalm 25:10, Exodus 20:6.
3. Those that are willing to forgive and show mercy to others. Matthew 5:7.
4. The righteous. 1 Kings 3:6.

5. Those that are willing to let go of the baggage from the past and move forward. Philippians 3:13.

6. Those that have faith in God and totally depend on Him. Not one leg in, one leg out. Psalm 32:10.

7. Those that fear God. Luke 1:50, Psalm 103:11.

8. The just such as Noah in the Bible. Genesis 6:9.

9. God's servants that walk holy before Him.

PRAYER

All evil attempts to pollute me through sex or food in my dream, in the name of Jesus, be aborted in fire.

Every evil attempt to paralyze me, spiritually or physically will not prosper in Jesus name.

Holy Ghost fire, scatter every destructive attempt made against me and my family, by anybody or power in Jesus name.

Lord, My life, rebel against evil attempts in the mighty name of Jesus.

All evil attempts to sabotage every good thing in my work throughout my life time, be

aborted in Jesus name

Father, show me the secrets of my life in Jesus name.

My father, according to your word in Jeremiah 33 v 3, show me the secrets behind every trouble in my life in Jesus name.

Dreams that will change my life for the better, manifest in Jesus name.

Holy Spirit, reveal to me my work environment, at the place I am living, working, etc. in Jesus name.

PROPHETIC DECLARATIONS

"I will pass through all thy flock to day, removing from thence all the speckled and spotted cattle, and all the brown cattle among the sheep, and the spotted and speckled among the goats: and of such shall be my hire" (Genesis 30:32)

Every Satanic regulating power that has caged your potentials by delaying the attainment of your set goals in life shall be hijacked by the spirit of God and reorganized to set you free, in the mighty name of Jesus Christ.

Every good dream of your life that has not come through shall be spiritually aided to come to fulfillment and reality, in the mighty name of Jesus Christ.

SECTION TWENTY (20):

GOD'S MERCY MANIFESTS IN MY LIFE

God's mercy manifests in various ways:

1. God's mercy manifest in His salvation plan for the redemption of man back to Himself. After all, He created man for His own pleasure!

2. God's mercy manifests in His forgiveness and His pardoning of our sins and iniquities. Numbers 14:19, Proverbs 28:13.

3. God's mercy manifests in his sending us Jesus as a man to live in our midst so that He can be an example to us as to how to live the Kingdom life.

4. God's mercy manifested in Jesus coming as a man so that He will be a High Priest that understands our infirmities and our human frailties and weaknesses. Hebrew 4:15.

5. The mercy of God is God's kindness in action. Psalm 51:1.

6. God's mercy secures our pardon from the wages of sin which is death. Romans 6:23, 1 Corinthians 15:10, Ephesians 2:4-5.

PRAYER

Breath of the Almighty, come upon all dry areas of my life in Jesus name.

According to Joel 2 v 25 – Anointing, Grace of God to recover my loses, envelop me now in Jesus name.

Every dry bone situation in my work, be turned around by fire in Jesus name.

I command the spring of ridicule targeted against me to dry up in the name of Jesus!

Every arrow of ridicule raised against me; be quenched in the name of Jesus!

I command the cycle of ridicule, mockery, and derision over my life to shatter unto desolation in the mighty name of Jesus!

The wrath provoking ridicule in my life; be silenced by the blood of Jesus in the name of Jesus Christ of Nazareth!

Thank you dear Lord God for giving me wisdom to overcome ridicule in the name of Jesus!

I am not feeble but strong in the Lord to overcome ridicule in the name of Jesus!

Holy Spirit encourage my heart against ridicule in the name of Jesus!

PROPHETIC DECLARATIONS

"And the man of God said, Where fell it? And he shewed him the place. And he cut down a stick, and cast it in thither; and the iron did swim." (2 Kings 6:6)

I decree today that any missing key in your life that requires urgent recovery shall be searched and found out until it is recovered by the mighty hands of God, in the mighty name of Jesus Christ.

When it is about the set time of Satan and any of his agents to strike bad in your home, heaven's alarm will sound to thwart their plans, in the mighty name of Jesus Christ.

SECTION TWENTY ONE (21):

LET THE MERCY OF GOD SPEAK FOR ME TODAY

(Exodus 33:19, 1 Corinthians 1:27, 1 Samuel 2:9)

BE MERCIFUL UNTO OTHERS AND THANK GOD FOR HIS MERCY

PRAYER

Lord, take over my life affairs in Jesus name.

Lord, wherever I have failed, take over in Jesus name.

Lord, wherever I am helpless and confused, take over in Jesus name.

Lord, whenever I need urgent help, take over in Jesus name.

Lord, wherever I need a touch of healing, take over in Jesus name.

Lord, in any way I need provision, take over in Jesus name.

Lord, wherever my family needs your settlement, take over in Jesus name.

Lord, in any area I must be restored take over in Jesus name.

Lord, by your power, make my life a wonder in Jesus name.

Lord, empower me for a new beginning in Jesus name.

PROPHETIC DECLARATIONS

Mathew 18 v 18 - “Verily I say unto you, whatsoever ye shall bind on earth shall be bound in heaven: and whatsoever ye shall loose on earth shall be loosed in heaven”

I reject defeat, shame and weeping this year in Jesus name.

I reject “Had I known” this year in Jesus name.

I reject Satanic attacks this year in Jesus name.

I reject contrary wind this year in Jesus name.

I reject mistakes and errors this year in Jesus name.

I reject Accident, Sudden death and calamities in Jesus name.

I reject Hardship, Delay and Frustration this year in Jesus name.

THIRD DIVISION: DEMANDING PRAYERS

SECTION ONE (1)

PRAYER FOR CHILDREN, YOUTH AND YOUR FAMILY

So they got into the city and killed everyone there. But they let that man and his whole family go free. (Judges 1:25b)

"The Ark of God remained there in Obed-edom's house for three months, and the LORD blessed the household of Obed-edom and everything he owned. (1 Chronicles 13:14)

Sing quality Praise and worship songs to the Almighty God.

1. I secure my family, precious ones, career, finances, enthronement and glory by the power in the blood of Jesus.
2. Evil powers calling my name for demotion and afflictions, die in the name of Jesus.
3. Evil incantations targeted against me, go back to senders by the power in the blood of Jesus.
4. Father, let every siege upon my life, family and destiny be broken and shattered to pieces in Jesus mighty name! (2 Kings 17:5-6).
5. I go free into blessings, fulfillment in life, family, ministry; fruitfulness and flourishing in Jesus mighty name! (Pray 3 times)
6. Every plan of death for my family, scatter in the name of Jesus.

7. Each member of my family will fulfill God's plan and purpose in Jesus name.

8. Father, let multitude of problems and antagonists be suddenly swept away in Jesus name (Isaiah 29:5).

9. Instead of harm, let there be divine preservation in Jesus name (Acts 28:6).

10. Evil plans against my family, die in Jesus name.

PROPHETIC DECLARATIONS

And I will make them and the places round about my hill a blessing; and I will cause the shower to come down in his season; there shall be showers of blessing (Ezekiel 34:26)

God will direct his showers of blessings upon your life's affairs today so much that every barren area of your life shall suddenly become fruitful, in the mighty name of Jesus Christ.

God shall arise for you to confront every opposition in your life so that whoever wishes for you to die before your time shall die in your stead, in the mighty name of Jesus Christ.

SECTION TWO (2):

DEALING WITH OPPORTUNITY WASTERS (2 Kings 5:1-27)

Prayer points

O Lord by your mercy, every opportunity I missed or wasted last year, bring them back to me by your mercy in Jesus name

Regain by the blood of Jesus, every ground I lost to my enemies last year in Jesus name

Failure at the edge of breakthrough, my life is not your candidate, die in Jesus name

Powers swallowing my Opportunities die in Jesus name

This year, every opportunity I have shall be fully maximized in Jesus name

Every spirit of rats and cockroaches attacking my destiny die in Jesus name

Spirit of greed and insensitivity that is making me loss opportunities die in Jesus name

My life attract and retain the blessings of God in Jesus name

Every giant standing against my good opportunities this year die in Jesus name

O Lord let me find favour in the place of every opportunity in Jesus name

Opportunities that will change my story and that of my family forever, let that opportunity locate me this year in Jesus name.

Every voice speaking against my Opportunities be silent and die in Jesus name

PROPHETIC DECLARATIONS

Which none of the princes of this world knew: for had they known it, they would not have crucified the Lord of glory (1 Corinthians 2:8)

Every organized defeat in your life shall be converted to supernatural victory in Christ Jesus, in the mighty name of Jesus.

Evil powers that stand to frustrate the saints of God shall never have dominion over any area of your life again in the mighty name of Jesus Christ.

SECTION THREE (3):

BREAKING THE YOKE OF STAGNANCY

John 5: 1-47

Prayer points

O Lord, have mercy on me in Jesus name

I break every yoke of stagnancy over every area of my life by the power in the name of Jesus

Every power tying me down to a spot, release me and die in Jesus name

My destiny, hear the word of the Lord, move forward by fire in Jesus name

Strong man supervising my stagnancy, what are you waiting for, die in Jesus name

Covenant of stagnancy entered into on my behalf or that I have entered into ignorantly, break by the blood of Jesus

Every collaboration of the powers of my father's house and the powers of my mother's house to stop my progress, scatter and die in Jesus name.

Father, by your thunder break every wall of stagnancy on my way this year in Jesus name

Powers assigned to stop me you are a failure, die in Jesus name

O Lord, let your power of revival and progress fall upon your church in Jesus name

Jesus arise and overshadow your church with your power

CONFESSION: This is my year of progress in all areas of my life in Jesus name

PROPHETIC DECLARATIONS

But I will send a fire upon Moab, and it shall devour the palaces of Kerioth: and Moab shall die with tumult, with shouting, and with the sound of the trumpet: (Amos 2:2)

May the Lord send his consuming fire over and upon every habitation of unrighteousness operating around and tormenting your life and destiny, in the mighty name of Jesus Christ.

Today, every Satanic strong tower of failure and limitation erected around your life, work, finance and your career shall be finally uprooted, in the mighty name of Jesus Christ.

SECTION FOUR (4):

FATHER CONNECT ME WITH MY DESTINY HELPERS

SCRIPTURES:

Psalm 121, Psalm 123, II Corinthians 1 v 24; Exodus 14 v 24 – 31;

Ruth 2, 3, and 4, Revelation 12 v 15 – 16; Psalm 116 v 5 – 7

EXHORTATION

1. Beloved, no one can run the race of life in isolation. You cannot be a lone ranger and fulfill your purpose of creation on the earth; we need each to live life to the fullest.

2. The agenda of God for us at redemption is a life of breakthrough, fruitfulness, abundance and help, but for all these to come to pass, there are ordained seasons, divine helpers and helps that we must connect with.

3. God is the ultimate source of help but He uses men as the means by which He sends the help our way. Life is about God linking you up with your divine helpers who will help you and not demand you for anything in return.

4. It is my prayer that the Lord will connect you with your destiny helpers this New Year in Jesus name.

PRAYERS

SCRIPTURE: Mathew 18 v 18 - "Verily I say unto you, whatsoever ye shall bind on earth shall be bound in heaven: and whatsoever ye shall loose on earth shall be loosed in heaven"

My divine helpers favour me by fire in Jesus name.

Every negative statement resisting my help, blood of Jesus, cancel them in Jesus name.

Every yoke of promise and fail in my life, break in Jesus name.

Blood of Jesus, link me up with my destiny helpers in Jesus name.

My divine helpers, dream of me by fire in Jesus name.

Help of God and Dew of help, locate me and rest upon me in Jesus name.

Goodness and mercy, locate my destiny helpers in Jesus name.

I will enjoy continuous help of God for ever in Jesus name.

PROPHETIC DECLARATIONS

And Israel saw that great work which the LORD did upon the Egyptians: and the people feared the LORD, and believed the LORD, and his servant Moses (Exodus 14:31)

As the Lord God of heaven lives, just as the children of Israel came out of Egypt without losing anyone in the land, the same way, the Lord will bring you out of every negative circumstance of your life without losing anything to the devil, in the precious name of Jesus Christ.

Every struggle and trouble of your life shall cease completely and you shall be free finally, in the mighty name of Jesus Christ.

SECTION FIVE (5):

WINNING BY THE BLOOD OF JESUS

Scriptural insight: Revelation 12:1-27

Prayer points

Jesus thank you for giving me victory through your blood on the cross of Calvary

Blood of Jesus purge my blood from every generational curses and afflictions in Jesus name

My blood receive deliverance by the blood of Jesus

Blood of Jesus speak for my favour this year in Jesus name

Blood of Jesus terminate every appointment my destiny have with death, failure and disappointments this year in Jesus name

Blood of Jesus wipe off every handwriting of evil from my life in Jesus name

This year I am marked with the blood of Jesus, evil and calamity shall pass over me in Jesus name

I purify my body, soul and spirit with the blood of Jesus for divine healing this year in Jesus name

Blood of Jesus silence every blood in my foundation crying for vengeance over my life in Jesus name

By the blood of Jesus I recover all that the enemies have stolen from me in Jesus name

By the blood of Jesus I stand against satanic order after my destiny in Jesus name

Blood of Jesus envelop all that pertain to me now in Jesus name

Confession: I secure my destiny and that of my family with the blood of Jesus

PROPHETIC DECLARATIONS

He revealeth the deep and secret things: he knoweth what is in the darkness, and the light dwelleth with him.(Daniel 2:22)

every Satanic point of contact into your life shall be exposed, condemned and destroyed by the power of redemption in Christ Jesus.

any stranger hiding in any part of your system and your finances in form of devourers, sicknesses and afflictions shall be flushed out by the blood of Jesus Christ, in the mighty name of Jesus Christ.

SECTION SIX (6):

DEALING WITH EVIL PLANTATION

Scriptural insight: Jeremiah 31: 1-40

Prayer points

Every evil plantation from my fathers' and mothers' house affecting my progress, die in Jesus name

O Lord visit the root of my life with the fire of the Holy Ghost in Jesus name

Evil plantation hidden within my life waiting to manifest on my glory die in Jesus name

Father uproot and burn to ashes every evil plantation in my life in Jesus name

Anything planted within me that has not manifested now but will manifest in future to make me backslide, dry up in Jesus name

Every root of sorrow in my life this year die in Jesus name

Every charm and enchantment in my foundation die in Jesus name

Every personality buried in my foundation tormenting my peace be silenced by the blood of Jesus.

Father let the root of my life be healed in Jesus name

I refuse to suffer what my parent has suffered in Jesus name

Plantation of darkness in my life die in Jesus name

I am redeemed by the blood of Jesus from every curse in my foundation in Jesus name

Confession: Evil growth in my body die in Jesus name

PROPHETIC DECLARATIONS

And he said, Take heed that ye be not deceived: for many shall come in my name, saying, I am Christ; and the time draweth near: go ye not therefore after them. (Luk 21:8)

as this day breaks, the mercy of the Lord will not allow you to be a victim in the hands of wrong people on the surface of the earth, in the mighty name of Jesus Christ.

I pray every form of deception around your life shall be exposed by the spirit of the Lord, in the mighty name of Jesus Christ.

SECTION SEVEN (7):

O LORD SHOW ME DIVINE BREAKTHROUGH DREAMS IN JESUS NAME SCRIPTURES

Mathew 13 v 25; Numbers 12 v 6; Gen. 28 v 10 – 16; 37 v 4 –

11; Acts 2 v 16 – 17; Job 33 v 14 – 16; Job 33 v 14 – 16

EXHORTATION

1. Dreams are spiritual media through which we receive information about happenings in the spirit realm. God Almighty created this medium in order to pass information to us His children. Every beneficial invention that mankind has ever come up with, is mostly received through the dream channel, but just like every good thing God created, Satan has perfected the art of polluting human destinies by planting evil seeds in people's lives through the medium of dreams.

2. Joseph's destiny was revealed to him through dreams. Gen. 37 v 4 – 11

3. Jacob's life transforming idea came through dream – Gen. 31 v 4, 10 - 13

5. Jesus Christ destiny was preserved and released for fulfilment through dream. Matthew 2 v 13; 19 – 23

6. Solomon received his wisdom through dream - 1 Kings 3 v 5 – 15

8. I pray that the Lord will show you divine breakthrough dreams in Jesus name.

PRAYERS

Lord my father, show me the secrets of my life in Jesus name.

My father, according to your word in Jeremiah 33 v 3, show me the secrets behind every trouble in my life in Jesus name.

Dreams that will change my life for the better, manifest in Jesus name.

Holy Spirit, reveal to me my work environment, the place I am living etc. in Jesus name.

Every operation of demotion in my dream, die in Jesus name.

Powers from the pit of hell, summoning my name before any dark mirror, die in Jesus name.

My "Joseph" dreams, hear the word of the Lord, manifest in Jesus name.

Anointing for victory in my dreams, fall on me in Jesus name.

Lord, show me what I need to know about my future/tomorrow in Jesus name.

Breakthrough provoking dreams, manifest in my life in Jesus name.

PROPHETIC DECLARATIONS

So they took up Jonah, and cast him forth into the sea: and the sea ceased from her raging (Jonah 1:15)

today, may the Lord arrest every troubler of your destiny for your own life and destiny to experience peace once and for all, in the mighty name of Jesus Christ.

may every rage of your enemies calm down peacefully from today, in the mighty name of Jesus Christ.

SECTION EIGHT (8):

GLORIFY YOUR NAME IN MY LIFE THIS YEAR

Scriptural insight: John 12: 1- 50

Prayer points

O Lord, I give you all the glory in the name of Jesus

Father, arise and glorify your name in my life this year in Jesus name

O Lord cover my nakedness with your glory in Jesus name

Glory of the living God, arise upon my life and announce my name for greatness in Jesus name

I shall excel above every unbeliever around me this year by the power in the name of Jesus

Crown of glory locate my head now in Jesus name

O Lord advertise your power in my life this year in Jesus name

Glory killers, my glory is not your candidate, therefore die in Jesus name

O Lord, let all that see me behold your glory in my life this year

Father let my light shine this year in Jesus name

Glory exchangers, my glory is not your candidate, die in Jesus name

Father, let every vile of darkness covering your glory in my life catch fire now in Jesus name

CONFESSION: Light of God possess my life this year in Jesus name

PROPHETIC DECLARATIONS

And shall not God avenge his own elect, which cry day and night unto him, though he bear long with them? (Luk 18:7)

this morning, all your silent and open prayers shall be heard of God until you are vindicated and be fully restored back to your lost dignity and position, in the mighty name of Jesus Christ.

and there shall be no more delays in answering your prayers and in solving your problems by the mighty hands of God, in the precious name of Jesus Christ.

SECTION NINE (9):

DEALING WITH MONITORING SPIRIT

Scriptural insight: Psalm 91: 1-16

Prayer points

Every demonic spirit from my father’s and mother’s house assigned to monitor my life, lose your hold upon my life in Jesus name

Strong man that my father's house and mothers house assigned against my marriage die in Jesus name

I separate my life and that of every member of my family from any ancestral bondage in Jesus name

Father let darkness over shadow the camp of every power monitoring my life in Jesus name

I destroy every communication gadget of the wicked over my life in Jesus name

O Lord make me invisible to my enemies in Jesus name

O Lord waste the wasters and destroy the destroyers assigned against my progress in Jesus name

Every power in the heavenlies against my life die in Jesus name

I refuse to cooperate with my enemies in Jesus name

Darkness following me about, scatter now in Jesus name

Fresh fire of the Holy Ghost possess my life now in Jesus name

I challenge the foundation of my life with the fire of the Holy Ghost in Jesus name

Confession: Familiar spirit of my father’s and mother’s house, my life is not your candidate die in Jesus name

PROPHETIC DECLARATIONS

Thus saith the Lord GOD, It shall not stand, neither shall it come to pass. (Isaiah 7:7)

as you wake up this morning, every arrow fired into your destiny in the night season by the wicked ones, shall be neutralised and returned to sender, and nothing glorious shall be delayed again in your life, so that you will always get things done at the right time, in the mighty name of Jesus Christ.

wherever the wicked ones are perpetrating their evil trade in your life shall be turned around for your glorious liberty, in the mighty name of Jesus Christ.

SECTION TEN (10):

I MUST ARISE AND SHINE

Scriptural insight: Isaiah 60:1-22

Prayer points

O Lord let my star shine this year in Jesus name

Power of darkness that want to cover my glory scatter in Jesus name

I frustrate every power against my shining this year in Jesus name

Plan of the wicked to put off my light scatter in Jesus name

Wind of the wicked assigned against my light scatter in Jesus name

Father I hid myself under your glory in Jesus name

Every demonic arrester assigned to arrest my star die in Jesus name

I command everything created by God to cooperate with my shining this year in Jesus name

Power assigned to take my life before my shining die in Jesus name

I receive the power to shine and show forth God's glory in this generation in Jesus name

Jesus take me out of the valley to my shining place in Jesus name

Jesus release your fire upon my life that will make me a shining star today in Jesus name

Confession: My destiny, hear the word of the Lord, arise and shine in Jesus name

PROPHETIC DECLARATIONS

And the songs of the temple shall be howlings in that day, saith the Lord GOD: there shall be many dead bodies in every place; they shall cast them forth with silence. (Amos 8:3)

i pray for you this morning that in every satanic temple where your name, your picture or any material from you is being manipulated for failure and afflictions, the lord shall arise for you to scatter them and put them in perpetual silence, in the mighty name of Jesus Christ.

and every altar and temple of satan, being hired to torment you and misdirect your purpose in life, shall come under the unquenchable fire of the holy ghost for instant consumption and final destructions, in the mighty name of Jesus Christ.

SECTION ONE (11):

DESTROYING THE POWER OF NIGHTMARE

Scriptural insight: Daniel 5: 1-31

Prayer points

Every power of the night assigned against my destiny, die in Jesus name.

My dream life, receive fire in the Jesus name.

Dream polluter, my life is not your candidate, die in Jesus name.

Blood of Jesus purge my dream life now in Jesus name.

Powers assigned to steal from me in the dream, die in Jesus name.

Every nightmare troubling my life, expire now in Jesus name

Every arrow fired into my dream life, backfire in Jesus name.

Every polluted food I have eaten that is tormenting me in the dream, I purge you now by the blood of Jesus

Power of my father's and mother's house troubling my dream life, die in Jesus name

Every power assigned to take my night vision away, die in Jesus name

Power using food and immorality to take my virtue in the dream die in Jesus name

O Lord arise and destroy that strongman of darkness monitoring my dream life in Jesus name

Confession: I cancel any evil dream that is waiting to happen in my life in Jesus name

PROPHETIC DECLARATIONS

If the iron be blunt, and he do not whet the edge, then must he put to more strength: but wisdom is profitable to direct (Ecclesiastes 10:10)

I pray this morning, that every weakness in your spiritual and physical operations in life shall be replaced with the wisdom of God for supernatural strength and all-time excellence, in the mighty name of Jesus Christ.

and you shall no longer operate below your maximum efficiency in any area of your life and destiny, in the mighty name of Jesus Christ.

SECTION TWO (12):

DELIVERANCE FOR THE CAPTIVES AND PROTECTION FROM VARIOUS ENEMIES INCLUDING HOUSEHOLD WITCHCRAFT

Confession:

The LORD will go forth like a warrior, He will arouse His zeal like a man of war. He will utter a shout, yes, He will raise a war cry. He will prevail against His enemies. (Isaiah 42:13)

Sing quality praise and worship songs to the Almighty God for at least 10 minutes.

1. Every witchcraft coven where my matters are being discussed, burn to ashes in the name of Jesus.

2. Every evil decision taken against me, go back to your senders in Jesus name.

3. Every agenda of death for me, die in Jesus name.

4. Divination and enchantments against me will not prosper in Jesus name.

5. Linkages to ancestral powers impacting my life negatively; break in the name of Jesus.

6. Ancestral sins will not destroy my future.

7. Every opening that has been allowing evil powers into my life and destiny, you will no more grant them access, be locked up by the blood of Jesus, in Jesus name.

8. I wipe off every evil ancestral mark from my forehead and every part of my body, soul and spirit by the blood of Jesus.

9. I come out of every cage of the enemy by the power in the blood of Jesus.

10. "It is written, I will contend with those who contend with you." Father, contend with and destroy every oppressor, strongman and power that has held me captive, that is holding me captive and wants to hold me captive in Jesus name. I go free from you by the power in the blood of Jesus.

PROPHETIC DECLARATIONS

The LORD God is my strength, and he will make my feet like hinds' feet, and he will make me to walk upon mine high places. (Habakkuk 3:19)

Just as Mordecai left the gate to take the exalted position of Haman in the king's cabinet, I decree upon you also that the force of uncommon favour will catapult you from your low estate to your high places in divine agenda, in the mighty name of Jesus Christ.

And may the wonders of the age answer to your personal efforts in righteousness until the name of the lord is being glorified, in the mighty name of Jesus Christ.

SECTION THREE (13):

DESTROYING THE EVIL ALTARS RAISE AGAINST MY DESTINY

Scriptural insight: Judges 6: 1-40

Prayer points

Every evil altar my parents have dedicated my, I command that altar to catch fire now in Jesus name

Evil family altar holding on to my virtues release my virtue and die in Jesus name

Demons attached to my life from that evil family altar, what are you waiting for die in Jesus name

Every power that has circulated my name on evil altar, fall down and die in Jesus name

Every like-father-like-son altar or like-mother-like-daughter altar in my lineage, my life is not your candidate release now in Jesus name

Every evil priest calling my name on evil altar catch fire with your altar in Jesus name

I refuse to answer the call of my name from evil altar in Jesus name

Every image representing or any member of my family on evil altar catch fire with your owner in Jesus name

I uproot every evil altar raised against my life in Jesus name

Altar of disfavour raised against me, be destroyed by the thunder fire of God in Jesus name

My name, jump out from the coven of the wicked and begin to do good in Jesus name

I render powerless every charm done on evil altar against my life in Jesus name

Confession: O Lord arise and destroy every evil altar battle with that area (name the area of your life your struggling with) in Jesus name

PROPHETIC DECLARATIONS

Whose fan is in his hand, and he will thoroughly purge his floor, and gather his wheat into the garner; but he will burn up the chaff with unquenchable fire. (Matthew 3:12)

This morning, I pray that every financial demon attached to your life and destiny, operating against your business and career, shall be detached and disconnected by the fire of the Holy Ghost, in the mighty name of Jesus Christ.

every charm and bewitchment running in parallel against the progress of your life, business and career shall be neutralized and rendered useless, in the mighty name of Jesus Christ.

SECTION FOUR (14):

GRACE FOR MY JOURNEY THIS YEAR

Scriptural insight: Romans 11: 1-36

Prayer points

O Lord I ask for grace to achieve the impossible this year in Jesus name

Father I desire more grace to obey you completely this year in Jesus name

Father give me the grace to walk deeper with you this year in Jesus name

O Lord let my flesh die in Jesus name

Grace to be steadfast in you Lord release upon my life now in Jesus name

Father release grace for deeper revelations and understanding of your word to me in Jesus name

O Lord let my Haman die in my place this year in Jesus name

Agreement of darkness over my faith, scatter and die in Jesus name

Father I receive grace for exploit in the work of the kingdom this year in Jesus name

I receive abundant grace to make great impact in this generation and beyond in Jesus name

O Lord fill my mouth with songs of praise this year in Jesus name

Power of the most high overshadow my life in Jesus name

Confession: King of Glory direct the affairs of my life this year in Jesus name

PROPHETIC DECLARATIONS

So they hanged Haman on the gallows that he had prepared for Mordecai. Then was the king's wrath pacified (Esther 7:10)

as you appear before the Lord in Zion this morning, I decree that the Lord shall arise for you so that whoever attempts to oppress your life and destiny in whatever capacity shall be brought under the terror of the Lord until you are finally set free, in the mighty name of Jesus Christ.

every Satanic and evil broadcaster of your success and breakthroughs shall be permanently silenced in the mighty name of Jesus Christ.

SECTION FIVE (15):

GREATER ACHIEVEMENT

1. Beloved, when you got born again, you were born to win and God's plan for you is perpetual victory. 2 Cor. 2 v 14 in Apostle Paul's word, the moment you get born again, you are a perfume of Christ knowledge in every place. Friend you are having victory for greater achievement, because you are appropriating the victory that is yours in Christ Jesus.

2. Greater achievement is explicitly chronicled in Psalm 113 v 7 – 8. It is an achievement that does not answer nor is dependent on anything or anyone, does not respect scarcity, not subjected to the whim and caprices of the storms of life.

3. Greater achievement is one that makes for domination, it empowers you to take your rightful position in the scheme of things and enables the carrier to walk upon his or her high places. Habakkuk 3 v 19. This shall be your portion this year in Jesus name.

4. As you pray the following prayers, you shall manifest greater achievement through this year and beyond in Jesus name.

5. Jesus is Lord!

PRAYERS

My ordained great achievement manifest in Jesus name.

My great achievement in any captivity, rebel, jump out and locate me in Jesus name.

This is my year of great achievement; I shall achieve and manifest greatness throughout this year in Jesus name.

My foundation will not sink my great achievement in Jesus name.

I shall manifest great achievement in all areas of my life this year in Jesus name.

I decree and declare that darkness will not overshadow my great achievement throughout this year and beyond in Jesus name.

My ordained great achievement for this year shall not be padlocked in Jesus name.

My great scheduled for this year, reject delay, calamities, drowning, downfall in Jesus name.

I decree, that any great achievement shall attract wealth/riches and prosperity in Jesus name.

By the help and mercies of God, this year I shall enlarge, break forth, expand, and cover new grounds in Jesus name.

Father, let kings stand at attention and princes bow low to me. Isaiah 49:7

Father, let kings and queens serve me, let them take care of all my needs. Isaiah 49:23

Lord, multiple every blessing in my hands.

PROPHETIC DECLARATIONS

And there was there with us a young man, an Hebrew, servant to the captain of the guard; and we told him, and he interpreted to us our dreams; to each man according to his dream he did interpret. (Genesis 41:12)

this morning, I pray that your name shall be remembered in quarters that matters so that your god-given provisions can be timely released and delivered into your hands, in the mighty name of Jesus Christ.

everywhere the cloud of shame has gathered against your life, the hands of God shall disperse it and it will never result into any rain of reproach for you, in the mighty name of Jesus Christ.

SECTION SIX (16):

FATHER, TAKE ME TO HIGHER GROUND

Scriptural insight: Psalm 23:1-6

Prayer Points

Father I thank you for your plan for me this year

Lord anoint me for divine lifting in Jesus name

Every strange hands pressing down my head, wither now in Jesus name

O Lord arise and deliver my head by fire in Jesus name

O Lord disgrace every power contending with my lifting in Jesus name

You my head and my feet, you shall not be bewitched in Jesus name

You my ladder to the top, appear now and take me to the highest mountain in Jesus name

Father, change my story for the best by fire in Jesus name

Every disease and affliction keeping me on the ground, hear the word of the Lord, disappear now in Jesus name

Every plantation of tail in my life, be uprooted and die in Jesus name

Father, surround my life with destiny helpers in Jesus name

Powers of my father's house and my mother's house, I am free from every curse of slavery in Jesus name

CONFESSION: Father, I am tired of the valley, take me to higher ground in Jesus name

PROPHETIC DECLARATIONS

So built we the wall; and all the wall was joined together unto the half thereof: for the people had a mind to work.(Nehemiah 4:6)

this morning, I decree that the glorious hands of the Almighty Father shall be stretched in your direction to partner with you in completing every project you have embarked upon, in the mighty name of Jesus Christ.

God of heaven will release his grace upon you that will enable you complete every process you have started in his name, in the mighty name of Jesus Christ.

SECTION SEVEN (17):

MY MIRACLE MANIFEST BY FIRE IN JESUS NAME

Scriptural insight: Act 3: 1-26

Prayer points

O Lord meet me at the point of my needs in Jesus name

Father, urgently manifest your miracle in my life in Jesus name

Any darkness in me against my miracles scatter in Jesus name

Father let my life be evidence of your great miracles in Jesus name

Father manifest your miracle in my job in Jesus name

Holy Ghost scatter every gathering against my miracles in Jesus name

Any voice against my miracles be condemned in Jesus name

My expected miracles this year manifest in Jesus name

My life shall be celebrated this year in Jesus name

Powers chasing miracles away from me be separated from me now in Jesus name

Father let my children be for signs and wonders in Jesus name

Father let your miracles in my life draw men to the kingdom of God in Jesus name

Confession: I connect my life to the socket of God working power in Jesus name

PROPHETIC DECLARATIONS

I have seen his ways, and will heal him: I will lead him also, and restore comforts unto him and to his mourners. Isaiah 57:18)

this morning, as the Lord lives, every silent discomfort in your life shall be taken away by the finger of God for supernatural comfort to register in your favour, in the mighty name of Jesus Christ.

whatever you have been struggling to get all this while, the grace of God shall bring it to you with relative ease, in the mighty name of Jesus Christ.

SECTION EIGHT (18):

FATHER REPAIR OUR FAULTY FOUNDATION

Ask God to open the eyes of His children to see their spiritual state

Ask for unity in the body of Christ all over the world. Acts. 2:1-5

Pray for pure and total repentance in the body of Christ Ps 51

Pray that people of God will be willing to wait on the LORD and renew their strength. Isaiah 40:28-31.

Pray that people of God will stop relying on their understanding. Prov. 3:5-6

Pray for right association for the children of God. Prov. 13:20

Pray that God will open the eyes of His Children to the importance of giving.3:9

Pray that God will help his Children to depart from wicked acts. Prov. 15:8

Pray that the fear of the Lord will rule the people of God .Prov.3:7-8

Pray for the heart to obey the great command Mark. 16:15-17

Pray that people of God will abide in Him. John 15:1-16

Ask God for the grace to love one another. John 15:17

Pray for the people of God to be people of integrity.

PROPHETIC DECLARATIONS

" I have been young and now am old yet have not seen the righteous forsaken, nor his seed begging bread." Psalm 37:25.

My Beloved, There may be lack in the land, but you shall not be pushed to want and penury.

You will not eat the food of your enemy.

God will not forsake you in whatever situation you find yourself.

Those planning to make jest of your downfall will end up celebrating your upliftment.

Today, God will send people that will make your dream come true into your life.

All your lacks shall be met with abundance in Jesus Mighty Name.

SECTION NINETEEN (19):

WAR AGAINST DESTRUCTIVE HABIT

Scriptural insight: Judges 16: 1-31

Prayer points

Every destructive habit designed to kill my glory die in Jesus name

Every destructive habit assigned to keep me in bondage die in Jesus name

Every internal bondage magnetizing the external bondage, break in Jesus name

I declare war against destructive habit assigned to ruin my life in Jesus name

I refuse to retire, I must refire in Jesus name

I bind the spirit of sexual immorality in Jesus name

I bind the spirit of Nollywood, Hollywood and Bollywood in my life in Jesus name

Every addiction to pornography die in Jesus name

Strength of God, empower me to say NO to every addiction from today in Jesus name

You my flesh, be nailed to the cross in Jesus name

My mind receive deliverance in Jesus name

My emotion receive the touch of God in Jesus name

Confession: I am free from every Satanic bondage of evil habit in Jesus name

PROPHETIC DECLARATIONS

The LORD shall fight for you, and ye shall hold your peace (Exodus 14:14)

by the mighty hands of the Lord, I decree today that every negative and contrary power, extending Satanic battles in your life shall be confronted, intercepted and overpowered by the spirit of the Lord, in the mighty name of Jesus Christ.

Whatever is trying to mock and ridicule the name of God in your life shall be in perpetual silence in the mighty name of Jesus Christ.

SECTION TWENTY (20):

COMMANDING THE MONTH FOR MY FAVOUR

Scriptural insight: Psalm 19:1-14

Prayer points

You heaven over my life this month be opened in Jesus name

My life shall command favour this month in Jesus name

Every evil on my way this month scatter in Jesus name

Evil gathering against my staff of bread this month scatter in Jesus name

Everything created by God cooperate with my destiny this month in Jesus name

Every witchcraft attack against my life this month backfire in Jesus name

This month let your peace overshadow my life in Jesus name

This month every opportunity on my way shall be maximized in Jesus name

O Lord promote me by fire this month in Jesus name

My going out and my coming in this month shall be blessed in Jesus name

I receive power to walk this month in victory in Jesus name

I receive grace to please God everyday of this month in Jesus name

Confession: Every power that want to challenge my favour this month shall be wasted in Jesus name

PROPHETIC DECLARATIONS

From henceforth let no man trouble me: for I bear in my body the marks of the Lord Jesus (Galatians 6:17)

this morning, I decree that god will put his mark of security and protection upon you for supernatural preservation of your life and all your properties, in the mighty name of Jesus Christ.

I decree that God will release covenant business and career insurers to work on your behalf, in the mighty name of Jesus Christ.

SECTION TWENTY ONE (21):

FRESH OUTPOURING OF THE HOLY SPIRIT AND REVIVAL

Joel 2:28, Acts 2:1-2.1 Corinthians 12:7-11, 2Timothy 1:6, 1st Corinthians 2:4Gal 5:22-23, Isaiah 37:31; Isaiah 32:15

PRAYER

Lord, let there be visible demonstrations of your power in my life and our services.

Lord, stir up every spiritual gift in my life that has become dormant or inactive.

Father, stir up every spiritual gift in the church that has been hidden or ignored.

Father, let there be divine investment of spiritual gifts and uncommon abilities in your church.

We begin to build for the Lord in the power of the Holy Spirit in the name of Jesus.

Father, reveal every broken wall in your church, in our families, businesses, career, ministry, etc.

We receive the power of God to begin to know what to do to build in the name of Jesus.

Father, pour out your Spirit upon your church and the body of Christ.

Father, refresh every thirsty soul.

Father, give me new depths of intimacy with the person of the Holy Spirit.

Father, anoint us as a church with fresh oil as we step into this season.

Father, let there be a sudden visitation of the Holy Spirit that will cause revival to break forth in your church.

Father, I decree that I am deeply rooted in your love and bear upward fruit.

Father, I decree that only the fruits of righteousness are made manifest in my life.

Father, empower me to win souls to the Kingdom of God daily.

PROPHETIC DECLARATIONS

Behold, I will do a new thing; now it shall spring forth; shall ye not know it? I will even make a way in the wilderness, and rivers in the desert (Isaiah 43:19)

this morning, I decree that every project in your hand that appears abandoned shall be bred upon by the Holy Ghost and highly favoured to resume again for successful completion, in the mighty name of Jesus Christ.

I prophesy strongly upon you today that natural disasters and synthetic calamities shall be far away from your home and habitations, in the mighty name of Jesus Christ.

SPECIAL PRAYERS

CONSECRATION

Joel 2:15-17, Romans 12:1-2

Iniquity is what can debar prayers from answering. Like Nehemiah sought the face of the Lord, seek the face of God for cleansing so as to approach the throne with confidence while making your requests known to God.

Father, consecrate me spirit, soul and body as a living sacrifice in Jesus name.

Father, I receive supernatural purging and cleansing from every dead work by the blood of Jesus.

Father, sanctify and purify me from the filthiness of the flesh and of the spirit. Malachi 3:3, Matthew 3:12

Father, I repent of every fault, every sin of my forefathers, of all their faults and misdeeds, please, forgive us in the name of Jesus.

Father, let there be restoration in the name of Jesus.

PRAYERS FOR OUR LEADERS, PASTORS AND PARENTS

Zechariah. 3:1-4, Isaiah 55:10-11, Numbers 23:19

Father, empower and anoint our leaders afresh on a daily basis.

Father, by your mercy, silence every evil plan against the ministry of our leaders. Psalm. 143:12

Father, fortify and strengthen our leaders. Isaiah 41:13-14

Father, divinely protect our leaders and their families. Psalm 125:2

Father, contend with those contending with our leaders and their families. Isaiah 49:24-26

Father, give our leaders and their families divine health. Psalm 128:3

Father, let your special hand of favour rest on our leaders for the rest of their lives. Psalm 27:1

Father, help our leaders to finish well and finish strong. 2 Timothy 4:6-8

Father, empower our leaders to break more new grounds this year in the name of Jesus.

Father, let your hand rest upon our leaders to operate in divine wisdom.

Father, continually fill our Pastors with the spirit of God and that they will not be distracted.

Father, by your grace and wisdom, distinguish our Pastors as pacesetters to lead us in your will.

Father, divinely protect them and their families. Cover them with the blood.

Lord, we pray our Pastors will hear you clearly through the Holy Spirit not emotions.

Father, remove every obstacle or objection from their path. John 12:37

PRAYER FOR ALL WORKERS AND MEMBERS

1. Father, increase our resources emotionally, spiritually, financially, intellectually and relationally. Ephesians 3:20
2. Father, we declare full expression of Your presence in all areas of our life. Zechariah. 2:5
3. Father, increase our capacity. Enlarge the coast of ministers, workers and members of your church.
4. Father God, increase our ABILITY – power to make things happen for Your Kingdom. 2 Samuel 22:34-36

5. Father, we declare divine protection on all our ministers, workers and members in your church. Psalm 91:10-11

REVIVAL AND RESTORATION IN THE LAND

1 Tim 1:18, 2 Chron. 7:14, Hosea 14:7, Zechariah 10:1/Ezekiel 37:1-14, Matt 16:18

Father, pour out your mercy on us as a church. Father, purge me of every form of disobedience and self-centeredness.

Father, give me the grace to make the sacrifices required for the revival to break forth in

our land.

Lord, we break down the satanic strongholds that control the minds and hearts of people

in the land.

Father, we release the spirit of prayer upon our land.

Father, build your church into strong army, to take territories for you.

Father, let there be restoration of lost hopes and dreams this year. 2 Samuel 9:7

Lord, I decree upon my life the anointing to overtake and recover lost glory. Joel 2:25-27, 1Samuel 30:8, 19

Father, make every dry land a spring of water for me and your church. Isaiah 35:7

Father, revive every dead situations in my life. Ezekiel 37

Father, release the spirit of grace and supplication upon your church to be a house of prayer and manifestation of your power.

Father, give your church grace (Leaders & Members) to be steadfast and faithful in their role in the land. Acts 6:4, 2 Corinthians 7:1, Galatians 6:9

Father, let there be oneness and unity in your church. Colossians 4:2, Philippians 2:2, 5, Matthew 16:18.

Father, build your church. We come against every agenda of the enemy against your church.

Father, let your church have a personal encounter with you.

Father, strengthen the faith of each member of your church to do the work of ministry. 2 Timothy 1:9, 1 Corinthians 16:13, Jude 1:20.

THE COMMUNITY – Acts 2: 46, 47

1. Father, grant us wisdom and strategy to minister/ be relevant to the community. Matt 5:16, Col 1:9-11

2. Lord, grant them receptive heart. Psalm 95:7-8, Acts 19:19-20
3. Father, grant us mighty signs and wonders.
4. Father, grant us power of the Spirit of God to preach the gospel in United Kingdom.

THE NATION – Jeremiah 29:7

1. Father, let your peace reign in our nation
2. Lord, let the storms of terror be removed. Psalm 91:4 –7, Mark 4:37 -39

3. Father, let the leaders surround and subject themselves to Godly counsel. Proverbs 19:21, I Timothy 2:1-2, Proverbs 14:34
4. Father, grant us boldness to declare and uphold the message of righteousness.

LEADERS

Lord, preserve and protect our leaders from the schemes and craftiness of men. Psalm 31:20

Father, strengthen our leaders as they face the challenges that come with responsibilities of leadership. Ephesians 3:16

Lord, give our leaders wisdom, knowledge and understanding for leadership. 1Samuel 2:35 & 1Chronicles 12:32

Father, release uncommon strategies and creative solutions to our leaders. Proverbs 8:12, Daniel 5:11-14

Lord, anoint our leaders with fresh oil. Psalm 92:10, Psalm 89:20

Lord, raise a hedge of protection around all Pastors, ordained ministers, leaders and their family.

Father, preserve leaders health and let them fulfill your counsel and mandate. Psalm 89:22-29, Psalm 91:9-16

PRAYER FOR MISSIONARIES, CHURCHES, HOMES AND MARRIAGES

Confession:

I looked for someone among them who would build up the wall and stand before me in the gap on behalf of the land so I would not have to destroy it, but I found no one. (Ezekiel 22:30)

For God was in Christ, reconciling the world to himself, no longer counting people's sins against them. And he gave us this wonderful message of reconciliation. (2 Corinthians 5:19)

Sing quality praise and worship songs to the Almighty God.

1. The plan of the enemy will not prevail over my life and family in Jesus name.

2. My family comes out of every cage and bondage of the enemy in Jesus name.

3. Arrows and shots fired at me and my family, go back to senders in Jesus name.

4. Father, perform your will in churches worldwide, save souls, establish and give hearts of disciples to all people in the nations in Jesus name.

5. Let churches grow, the kingdom of God populated and the kingdom of darkness depopulated in Jesus name.

6. Lord, let there be revival in my life, family and community in Jesus name.

7. The powers of hell and death will not prevail against the churches in Jesus name.

8. Father, increase your churches on all fronts in Jesus name.

9. Father, let the church be willing and obedient to work in Your way and will, to allow You confirm Your signs and wonders, in Jesus name.

10. Demonic forces hindering the growth and advancement of God's kingdom, your time is up, I challenge you by the blood of Jesus and the Holy Ghost fire, die in Jesus name.

11. Let all nations and people begin to flow into churches in Jesus name (Isaiah 2:2-3).

12. Lord, let there be dedicated, committed and faithful disciples in your churches in Jesus name.

13. Let each member of the body of Christ walk in their offices and divine appointments in Jesus name (Joel 2:7, 1 Corinthians 12:28).

14. Let ministers be faithful, committed and loyal in Jesus name.

15. Lord, help the ministers and missionaries to fulfill their calling in Jesus name.

16. Take your personal prayer points.

17. Thank you Lord for answered prayers.

PRAYER FOR SHINING, EXCEPTIONAL FAVOR, ADVANCEMENT AND PROMOTION

Confession:

The king then removed his signet ring (the very one he had taken back from Haman) and gave it to Mordecai. And Esther designated Mordecai to be in charge of Haman's estate. (Esther 8:2)

Sing quality Praise and worship songs to the Almighty God for at least 10 minutes.

1. Lord, give me an excellent spirit that will catapult my rising in the mighty name of Jesus.

2. Lord, let your favor distinguish me in Jesus name.

3. Father, put a clear difference between those who serve you and those who do not.

4. Lord, let this year be my year of answered prayers and dumbfounding miracles in Jesus name.

5. I take back my ring of authority from every Haman around me in Jesus name.

6. My antagonists will be stepping stones to my greatness and promotion after the order of Daniel.

7. As the King sent his word, loosed Joseph and established him as the governor of the land, by the Word of God, I am loosed from every captivity and established in my esteemed God ordained throne in Jesus name.

8. Every pain of the past be wiped off by the blessings and joy of my present and future after the order of the Manasseh blessing in Jesus name.

9. Where I have been afflicted, I will become fruitful and progressive after the order of Ephraim blessings, in Jesus name.

10. I will not die before or on my day of glory. I will live to enjoy my higher next levels in Jesus name.

11. Father, let divine revelation, insight and closeness to the Holy Spirit advance me. (Genesis 41:39)

12. Father, in any way the enemy has gained a way into my life, in your mercy, close it up and repair my destiny in line with your will in the mighty name of Jesus.

13. Father, let failure be turned to success in every area of my life, family, career, ministry and destiny in Jesus name.

14. Lord, for me, let there be advancement from backwardness to the front-lines in Jesus name.

15. I will not die, I will live and gloriously fulfill God's purpose in this year and beyond in Jesus name.

PRAYERS FOR OUR CHURCH

Nehemiah 2, 4, 6; Ezra 4,5,6; Mathew 16 v 18 – 19; Jer. 1 v 1 – end; Col. 2 v

14-15; 1 Cor. 16 v 9; 2 Cor. 1 v 9 – 10

CONFESSION

Psalm 50:15 "And call upon me in the day of trouble; I will deliver thee and thou shall glorify me"

PRAYERS

Praise and worship unto the Lord for He is the Mighty man in charge of our church Congregation and personal repentance to be carried out.

Ask for mercy and grace, plead the blood of Jesus for cover you, your family and our church Thank God on behalf of the Church on the following:

For founding the Ministry our church in the Power of the Holy Ghost

For His mercy, glory upon the Senior Pastor and his family

For how far God has helped you and the Ministry

For all the great testimonies since the inception of the Church

For frustrating the tokens of the liars and defeating our enemies.

For His revelation knowledge and anointing on the Ministry our church to fulfilling His promise that He will build the Church and the gate of hell shall not prevail.

Rebuke and overthrow all Territorial Spirit (over the area where our church is located) manifesting as OCCULTISM, Religious Deception, Prostitution

Command all Satanic Altars fashioned against our church and other genuine ministries in the environment scatter by fire in Jesus name.

Every witchcraft and occultism stronghold against our church be pulled down in Jesus name.

Every witchcraft programme against you, be destroyed in Jesus name.

Every power using evil rosary, evil mat, evil incense, ritual, sacrifices against the church die by fire in Jesus name.

Powers/Agents, using the sand to consult against our church Dust of the Earth, battle them to nothing in Jesus name.

Satanic agents, who have entered into covenant of death against our church) and her members die by your covenant in Jesus name.

PRAYERS FOR THE BODY OF CHRIST

SCRIPTURES

Phil. 2 v9 – 11; Eph. 6 v 10 – 18; Mathew 18 v 18 – 20

EXHORTATION

The body of Christ needs prayer, and we as part of the Church need to arise and cry unto God for her so that the Church will not cease to be relevant in this generation. We have to pray that God will empower the Church universally in order to triumphantly march over the kingdom of darkness and establish righteousness in every nations of the world.

PRAYERS

Lord, protect your interest in all your Churches all over the world and let no corruption enter the Church in Jesus name.

Let every host of darkness that is assigned against the body of Christ for calamity, be scattered and rendered powerless in Jesus name.

Let every activity of hell be destroyed over the body of Christ in Jesus name.

Let unity, love, righteousness, truth and holiness prevail and reign in the body of Christ in Jesus name.

We pray for global harvest of souls and true revival in the body of Christ so as to be able to reach the unreached in Jesus name.

Lord, send more faithful labourers and raise genuine ministers for your kingdom work in Jesus name.

Lord, empower all the true ministers of the gospel and keep them from compromise and perils of the end time in Jesus name.

Let every weapon of darkness against the body of Christ and expansion of his kingdom on earth, be destroyed in Jesus name.

Holy Spirit of God, take over every activity of your Church on earth like the day of Pentecost in Jesus name.

Lord God, keep our church till the end and let not the will and plan of Satan prevail over the Church, the set man, his family, the ministers and every member of the Ministry in Jesus name.

NUMERICAL GROWTH

Micah 4:1-2, 1 Tim 1:18, Ps 2:8, Ezekiel 36:10, 11, 30, 37

1. Father, give your church burden for lost souls.

2. Father, uncover every veil hindering people to receive the glorious light of the gospel.

3. Father, we call forth those who are appointed to be the sons and daughters of your church.

PRAY FOR HARVEST OF SOULS

Father, let there be massive inflow of souls in all our parishes. Isaiah 2:2-3

Father, increase the influence of your churchin the community that God has called her to. Isaiah 2:2-3

Father, show me divine opportunities to win souls to His Kingdom

HEALING & HEALTH – Isaiah 53:5

Father, illuminate my eye with the revelation of Christ's finished work. Isaiah 53:4-5, 1st Peter 2:24

Lord, cast out every spirit of infirmity. Mark 7:25-30, Luke 13:11-13

Lord, I will enjoy perfect health and wholeness. Isaiah 58:8, Jeremiah 30:17

Father, no room in my life for sorrow, depression sickness and pain. Isaiah 53:4

Father, I declare that every sickness in my body is destroyed in Jesus name. 1 John 3:8.

SINGLE PERSONS

Father, release your blessings upon the lives of our singles. Matthew 6: 33, Ex 23:25, Colossians 3: 23-24
Father, let our singles be preferred above their mates.
Father, no longer shall the singles be overlooked, desolate or rejected. Daniel 6:3, Esther 2:9, 1 Peter 2: 9
Father, let wisdom, knowledge and understanding lead them into favour in the sight of God and man. Isaiah 11: 2-3, Malachi 3:14-18

FINANCIAL BREAKTHROUGH and CAREER, BUSINESS

Father, give me an excellent spirit after the order of Daniel. Proverbs 22:29, Proverbs 10:4, Daniel 6:3-4
Father, favour me and the work of my hands beyond my imagination. Psalms 5:12, Luke 2:52

Lord, give me talents and business ventures that will make room for me. Proverb 18:16, Genesis 26:22

PROTECTION

Father, protect me, my family and Church form tragedies and calamities. Philippians 1:6

Lord, hide me in the hollow of your hand. Isaiah 51:16, Psalm 17:8
Father, keep me from evil and protect me. I come against sickness and disease. Psalm 91

Lord take away sickness from the midst of your church. Exodus 23:25

DIRECTION

Father, give me grace to complete the project/assignment/ministry you committed into my hands. Acts 20:24.
Father, grant me divine speed this year. Habakkuk 3:19
Father, grant me divine wisdom and clear direction. Isaiah 30:21

JOY

Father, cause me to sing songs of everlasting joy. Isaiah 35:10
Lord, let sorrow, sighing and mourning flee far away from me. Isaiah 35:10

Father, from now, let me know only the joy of The Lord continually.
Father, let me enjoy joy unspeakable and fill my life with your glory throughout

OPEN THE FLOODGATE OF HEAVEN

Father, please release the flood of righteousness. Psalm 51 Father, release the flood of your Power, Victory, and peace to our entire nation.

Father, help me to obey your word. Father, help me to obey your voice. Father, let the nations of the earth be blessed through me, Zechariah. 10:1

Father, in a special way, do something new in our lives.

PEACE

Father, please give me peace like a river in every facet of life. Isaiah 66:12

Father, let your peace rule in all areas of my life Father, still every storm in my life, Mark 4:39

DIVINE DIRECTION AND STRATEGY

Isaiah 48:17, John 10:4-5, Isaiah 30:21, Psalm 37:23

1. Father, I declare that my ears will hear the voice of God clearly.

2. Father, I download heavenly strategies to establish dominion in my life.

3. Lord, order every step of members.

4. Father, I move from glory to glory to fulfill God's purpose for my life.

SUPERNATURAL ABUNDANCE

Father, open our eyes to the principle of abundant life and fruitfulness. Proverb. 3:5 – 10

Lord, anoint your people to multiply greatly. According to your word, Lord Jesus, make your church exceedingly fruitful. Genesis 12:1 – 3, Genesis 26:12 – 13, Genesis 30:43, Genesis 28:3 – 4

Father, bless us 'O LORD, send the arrow of barrenness back to the sender. Genesis 27:27 – 29, Genesis 12:3

FINANCES

Father, make us more fruitful this year. John 15:2 Declare a divine change of status in every area of your life. Genesis 32:28

Declare to God that you will not let Him go unless He blesses you. Genesis 32:26

Pray against financial death and bankruptcy, for financial promotion in the life of members. Psalm.1:3

PRAYER FOR MISSIONS

1. Thank God for strength, grace and daily provision – Nehemiah 8:10
2. Pray that that Lord almighty shall give fresh unction to carry on the work – I John 2:20.
3. Pray that the beauty of the Lord shall rest upon the leaders and their families – Psalm 90:17.
4. Pray for excellent spirit and pray against every evil plans their work – Daniel 6:3; 2 Corinthians 10:4-5.

DARKNESS FADE AWAY

Scriptural insight: Genesis 1: 1-31

Prayer points

Every darkness in me and around me scatter in Jesus name

Jesus the Light of the world, lighten my path this year and do not allow me to stumble by your power

Powers hiding in the dark to afflict my life be exposed and disgraced in Jesus name

Every altar of darkness in my father's house and mother's house, catch fire now in Jesus name

I break every association with darkness by the blood of Jesus Christ

Every darkness in my place of work and my habitation fade away now in Jesus name

I command darkness to overshadow the camp of my enemies in Jesus name

My glory in the cage of darkness come out now and shine in Jesus name

I nullify every judgment of kingdom of darkness against my household in Jesus name

Glory of the living God possess me and announce my name for good in Jesus name

Every satanic police assigned to arrest my glory, catch fire and die in Jesus name

Check point of darkness assigned to stop my progress, scatter now in Jesus name

CONFESSION: Darkness, hear the word of the Lord, depart from me now in Jesus name

UNITY OF THE BODY OF CHRIST

Scriptural insight: John 17:1-26

Prayer points

Father I thank you for the gift of Holy Spirit to your church

Jesus I thank you for your continuous prayers for the church

Any satanic agents assign against the unity and progress of your church, die in Jesus name

Environmental powers against the unity and peace of your church, die in Jesus name

Father let your power for signs and wonders fall upon your church in Jesus name

O Lord prosper your church by fire in Jesus name

Every demonic agents on assignment against your church, catch fire in Jesus name

O Lord increase and enlarge your church now in Jesus name

Father make your church a solution ground in Jesus name

O Lord glorify your name in all our programmes this year in Jesus name

O Lord send us revival in your church now in Jesus name

Every assignment of darkness against your church, scatter in Jesus name

CONFESSION: My life arise and shine in Jesus name

PRAYER OF INTERCESSION FOR BRETHREN

Scriptural insight: James 5: 1-20

Prayer points

Thank God for of every thing

O Lord arise and manifest yourself in the life of every member of this church in Jesus name

Father, wipe away every tears from the eyes of every member of church in Jesus name

Jesus make this year, a year of multiple blessing and favour for everyone in this church

Every single person in our midst seeking your face for their own God given partner (Husband or wife), Father settle them speedily this year in Jesus name

Every family in this church trusting you for the fruit of the womb, Father answer them speedily this year in Jesus name

Father, every member of this church having immigration issues and trusting you for their own settlement in this land, Lord intervene and settle them in Jesus name

Every member of this church with long term illness and diseases, I command that fellow to be healed in Jesus name

Father, we commit every marriage experiencing shame and discomfort or even at the point of break up, Lord intervene in these marriages in Jesus name

Every home under attack, I command that attack to go back to sender in Jesus name

Every embargo upon the success of our children in your church is lifted now in Jesus name

Father for everyone inyour church looking for job or willing to change his/her job, Lord give them job that will glorify your name in Jesus name

CONFESSION: We shall celebrate and testify this year in Jesus name

PRAYER FOR CHILDREN

Scriptural insight: Mathew 19: 1-30

Lord, let our children receive life and they shall be saved. 2 Timothy 3:15, Titus 1: 9

Father, may our children never be victims of someone else's mistake.

Lord, our children's destinies will not be destroyed or disrupted by accident or incident.

Father, our children's lives will not be terminated as a result of someone's error. 2Samuel 4:4, 2 Peter 3:17

Pray for growth and increase in wisdom, stature and favour with God and man in the lives of our children. Luke 2: 52, 2 Peter 3: 18, 92:12

Father, we thank you for the life of all our children

Every power assigned to draw my children away from the presence of God, you are liar die in Jesus name

I break every inherited curses and afflictions by the blood of Jesus in the life of my children in Jesus name

God of purpose and destiny, empower my children to fulfil their destinies in Jesus name

O Lord put your fear and love in the heart of my children in Jesus name

CONFESSION: My children shall be for undeniable signs and wonders in Jesus name

PRAYER FOR OUR SPIRITUAL LEADERS

Pray for peace in the health of our spiritual leaders

Pray for more physical strength for our spiritual leaders

Pray that God will favour the family of our spiritual leaders with divine health.

Pray that the hand of the Lord will be upon our spiritual leaders to out run the Ahab that is working against their ministry.

Pray that every cloud of darkness that may be gathering around the ministerial assignment of our spiritual leaders should disappear for the light to prevail

Pray that no secret of the enemy shall be hidden in the lives, home and ministries of our spiritual leaders

Pray that God will surround our spiritual leaders' family as mountains surround Jerusalem. Ps.125:2

Lord, preserve and protect our leaders from the schemes and craftiness of men. Psalm 31:20
9. Father, strengthen our leaders as they face the challenges that come with responsibilities of leadership. Ephesians 3:16
10. Lord, give our leaders wisdom, knowledge and understanding for leadership. 1Samuel 2:35 & 1Chronicles 12:32

PRAYER FOR OUTREACH

Give all the glory to God for the reality of the power of resurrection. Matt. 28:1-4.

Thank God for using this program to populate His kingdom. Acts. 2:37-47.

Pray for more strength for all our Pastors, Ministers and workers, that God will use them mightily more. Deut.33:25; Josh.14:11; 1Chron.29:12; Josh. 14:9.

Pray for divine visitation in all our church all over the world. Ps.111:9; Ps.113:9-10; Jer.20:113; Gen.49:25.

Pray for the purpose of God to be established in the life of God's children in this program.Eccl.8:6; Rom.9:1; Eph.1:11.

Ask God to deliver every captive of the mighty.Isa.49:24-26.

Pray for full restoration in all our programPs.126:1-6.

Commit the Engineering department, Choir, Ushers, Prayer Warriors and other workers in the church into the hands of God in all programs.

Pray against the kidnappers, ritual killers and armed robbers. Ps.124:6 Prov. 15:30.

Pray for your Pastors, Ministers, Workers and yourself.

PRAYER FOR FAMILY

Scriptural insight: Colossians 3: 1-25

Prayer points

Every power sitting on the prosperity of my marriage die in Jesus name

Every power against my marital peace and joy fashioned against my home die in Jesus name

Counsel of the wicked against my spouse and my children shall not stand in Jesus name

Powers assigned to turn the back of my family against me die in Jesus name

Favour of God envelop my home in Jesus name

This year the testimonies of my home shall be evidence to all in Jesus name

I break every siege over the affairs of my home in Jesus name

Father, let your power of increase fall upon our finances this year in Jesus name

Every power against the unity of my home die in Jesus name

Arrows of sorrow and disappointment fashioned against my home back fire in Jesus name

11 Any Jezebel or Pharaoh against my home shall die by fire in Jesus name

12 Blood of Jesus be the umbrella over my home in Jesus name

CONFESSION: My home shall be the dwelling place of the Holy Ghost in Jesus name

PERFECT YOUR PROMISES IN MY LIFE

Scriptural insight: II Peter 1: 1-21

Prayer points

O Lord, let your thought of peace that will give me that expected end be perfected in my life this year in Jesus name – Jeremiah 28:11

Father, let every handwriting of evil ordinances that against me be nailed to the cross in Jesus name – Colossians 2:14

Jesus I receive the baptism of the Holy Spirit now in Jesus name - Act 1: 8

O Lord deliver me and my household from the snare of the fowler, the noisome pestilence, the terror of the night, arrow that flieth by day, pestilence that walketh in darkness and the destruction that wasted at noonday this year – Psalm 91: 3-6

I am free from every bondages and slavery this year in Jesus name – John 3:36

Father, arise and fight for me now and restore my peace in Jesus name – Exodus 14:14

Lord I receive grace to be a kingdom investor so that I will receive my reward of prosperity – Proverb 11:25

I and the children the Lord has given me shall be for signs and wonders this year in Jesus name – Isaiah 8:18

O Lord by your divine wind, direct the prosperity of the wicked to me this year in Jesus name – Proverb 13:23

O Lord envelop me and my household with your favour this year in Jesus name – Proverb 3:4

CONFESSION – Move my life forward by fire in Jesus name

STORM BE STILL

Scriptural insight: Mark 4:1-41

Prayer points

Every storm ragging against my job be still now in Jesus name

Inherited storm of my father and mother's house affecting my greatness I command you to be ceased now in Jesus name

Father empower me to walk through every storm in this year in Jesus name

I rebuke every storm assigned to take away your glory in my life in Jesus name

Every storm in my life that has made me a slave of fear. I command the storm and the fear to die in Jesus name

Peace of the living God overshadow my life in Jesus name

Every storm that want to swallow my life this year, die in Jesus name

I command every storm assigned against me this year to locate the camp of my enemies in Jesus name

Every power behind any storm against me this year I command you to die in Jesus name

Every storm assigned to scatter your church you are a liar die in Jesus name

Confession: O Lord take me to your desired destination for my life this year in Jesus name

I SHALL NOT LABOUR IN VAIN THIS YEAR

Scriptural insight: Luke 5:1- 39

Prayer points

I destroy every power harvesting my good reward in Jesus name

Powers that want me to work hard and die a pauper you are a liar die in Jesus name

Spirit of error assigned to turn my reward to reproach, you are a liar die in Jesus name

In this year I refuse to invest my resources in things that will not prosper my life in Jesus name

Any bewitchment over my staff of bread, die in Jesus name

Father, let me experience your net breaking prosperity this year in Jesus name

Every evil basket assigned against my finances catch fire in Jesus name

My name in the evil pots of non-achievement, jump out now in Jesus name

I rebuke every demonic power programme to drain my resources this year in Jesus name

I soak all my resources in the blood of Jesus and I shall not suffer loose this year in Jesus name

O Lord let your favour envelop my labour in Jesus name

I receive the power to get wealth this year in Jesus name

Confession: Holy Ghost empower me to prosper this year in Jesus name

THAT I MAY KNOW HIM

Scriptural insight: Philippians 3:1-21

Prayer points

Jesus I thank you for the gift of salvation of my soul and the world at large

Lord every spirit of lukewarmness and backsliding that has followed me into this year, let them die now in Jesus name

O Lord purge my heart by the fire of the Holy Ghost in Jesus name

Holy Spirit I shall cooperate with you fully this year in Jesus name

Lord I crucify my flesh to the cross today in Jesus name

Holy Spirit open my eyes to the deep revelation and understanding of your word in Jesus name

O Lord I cry for abundant grace to tarry more in the place of prayer this year in Jesus name

Every material of the old nature in my custody that is drawing me back to my vomit

I release you now and die in Jesus name

Holy Ghost sanctify my life by your fire in Jesus name

Father I need you every second all the way this year in Jesus name

Every act of worldliness in me, die in Jesus name

Lord open my eyes to see clearly and my ears to hear you clearly in Jesus name

Confession: Father, take me deeper in you this year by your grace in Jesus name

LORD DELIVER MY FOUNDATION

Scriptural insight: Psalm 11: 1-7

Prayer Points

The foundation of life receive deliverance by fire now in Jesus name

O Lord deliver my blood now in Jesus name

Every witchcraft power in my foundation die in Jesus name

Every blood crying from my foundation against my destiny die in Jesus name

Evil covenant in my foundation, holding me captive break by the blood of Jesus

Evil words in my foundation that is affecting my progress die in Jesus name

Seeds of evil in my foundation, my life and that of my family shall not be harvested by you in Jesus name

Every occult power in my foundation laying hold on my life, you are a liar die in Jesus name

Every wickedness of the wicked from my foundation die now in Jesus name

Every curse from my foundation that is contending with the plan of God for my life die in Jesus name

Every evil associated with my father and mothers house, my life is not your candidate die in Jesus name

Fire of the Holy Ghost purge my foundation in Jesus name

Confession: Jesus is my sure foundation and on Him I stand and build my life

WAR AGAINST HOUSEHOLD WICKEDNESS

Scriptural insight: Genesis 37: 1-36

Prayer points

Every association of the powers of my father's house and my mother's house scatter in Jesus name

Every familiar personality and power consulting the herbalist for my sake carry your evil load now in Jesus name

Household wickedness attacking my prosperity die in Jesus name

O Lord scatter the language of household wickedness against my progress in Jesus name

Every concluded work of household powers to turn my life to rag die in Jesus name

O Lord avenge me of the household wickedness in Jesus name

Household powers oppressing my life , enough is enough die in Jesus name

Strong man of my father's house monitoring my life die in Jesus name

I reject the covenant of suffering and tail in my father and mother's house in Jesus name

I recover all my treasures in the custody of the household witchcraft now in Jesus name

My virtues in the custody of the household witchcraft be release now by fire in Jesus name

Any bewitchment against my life backfire in Jesus name

Confession: Fire of the Holy Ghost consume every unrepentant household witchcraft against my life in Jesus name

INFIRMITY MUST DIE

Scriptural insight: Luke 43:1 - 56

Prayer points

Every satanic inflicted diseases in my life die in Jesus name

I command the source of my illness to dry up now in Jesus name

Every long term infirmity in my life die in Jesus name

O Lord touch me and make me whole now in Jesus name

Arrow of infirmity fired into my life backfire now in Jesus name

My head reject infirmity this year in Jesus name

O Lord let me enjoy all round rest this ear in Jesus name

Any infirmity assigned into my life to make me a pauper, you are a liar die in Jesus name

Inherited infirmity my life is not our candidate die in Jesus name

O Lord arise and destroy any seed of infirmity in my life in Jesus name

My body hear the word of the Lord, be purged now in Jesus name

Confession: My body is the temple of the Holy Ghost, therefore any stranger in my body come out now in Jesus name

JESUS BAPTISE ME WITH HOLY GHOST AND FIRE

Scriptural insight: Matthew 3:1-17

Prayer points

O Lord baptize me with your Holy Ghost and fire in Jesus name

Father let the mantle of the prophet be released upon my life in Jesus name

Jesus let the fire of the Holy Ghost purge my spirit, soul and body in Jesus name

Fire of the Holy Ghost fall upon me for my deliverance today in Jesus name

My garment of Shane catch fire now in Jesus name

Father empower me for extra ordinary achievement this year in Jesus name

I burn into Ashes by the fire of the Holy Ghost every habitation of wickedness against my destiny in Jesus name

Father make me undisputable channel of blessing to your Kingdom and to my generation this year in Jesus name

Anointing that cannot be insulted fall upon me now in Jesus name

This year my case is completely different because I have been empowered by God to prosper in Jesus name

I receive power to win souls to the kingdom of God this year in Jesus name

I receive power to work miracles in the name of Jesus

Confession: In the name of Jesus from today I begin to walk above the natural by the power of the Holy Ghost

FIGHTING WITH THE FINGER OF GOD

Scriptural insight: Daniel 5: 1-31

Prayer points

Thou Finger of God , arise and fight my battle in Jesus name

Finger of the living God, contend with every power of darkness contending with my breakthrough in Jesus name

Lord my father, rewrite my story for good with your Finger this year in Jesus name

I cancel every agreement of darkness over my life with the Finger of God in Jesus name

O Lord lift me up by your Finger in Jesus name

Thou Finger of God perform your wonders in my life in Jesus name

Father, write your laws in my heart by your Finger in Jesus name

O Lord open my heaven with your Finger and let it never be close again in Jesus name

God of Elijah, arise with your Finger and appear in my situation by fire in Jesus name

O Lord, let your Finger command my destiny in the name of Jesus Christ

Thou Finger of God return every arrow fired against my life back to sender in Jesus name

Finger of God scatter the coven of darkness against my life in Jesus name

Confession: Thou Finger of God write the obituary of the powers of my father's house and my mother's house this year in Jesus name.

ABOUT THE AUTHOR

Joel Odunayo Daramola whom God raised from grass to grace, has pioneered many parishes in The Redeemed Christian Church of God.

Currently: As Assistance Provincial Pastor Admin in Lagos province 37.

A graduate of The Redeemed Christian Bible College (RCBC), School of Disciple (SOD) and Institute of Leadership.

He holds a B.A. (Ed) in Guidance and Counseling from the prestigious University of Lagos (UNILAG).

He is a teacher who is registered with the teacher's registration council of Nigeria (TRCN)

A trained R & A Engineer (thermodynamics) with over 30 years' experience.

He is the CEO, Ayo-Technical Services (ATS). & Vision Link For You and I.

He is the host of Power Service (a weekly breakthrough and deliverance service) for over two decades.

A prolific writer, author of many books; a respected Evangelist, a gifted prophet with vast insight into the word of God.

Publisher of the Monthly Journal: "VISION LINK" for more than 20 years.

He has the vision to challenge young people to actualize their potentials in life.

His mandate is to spread the word of God, raise disciples, and build them to maturity for the perfection of saints through God's empowerment.

A prolific speaker, dexterous writer and a leading voice in Ministry and Leadership circles,

He is sought as a Conference speaker across the globe. His ministry is in high demand by both denominational and non-denominational ministries alike as his ability to engage people with God's word and effective prayer

He is passionate about raising people who are thoroughly steeped in Kingdom values and very relevant in the Secular world.

He believes that Christians should be able to influence society with kingdom principles.

His fine blend of excellence and spirituality has made him stand out from the pack.

He believes God has a plan for everybody and that God can take the most unlikely and use him powerfully.

A Youth leader, an administrator, entrepreneur and motivational speaker with a global vision.

A motivational speaker for over two decades. He has organized seminars and conferences to inspire the Youths in schools and Church for Nation building, Vision discovery and career advancement. His fine blend of excellence and spirituality has made him stand out from the pack, he believes that God has a plan for everybody and that God can make use of anyone powerfully.

He has published many books; Sounds of the abundance of rain; At the darkest hour; Are you passing through? Destined for greatness but tied down among others.

He is happily married to Pastor (Mrs.) C.O. Daramola and their union is blessed with four Children: Power, Queen, Excellence and Great.

Emails: pastordara@yahoo.com & visionlinkdara1@gmail.com

Phone & WhatsApp +2348033275896.

Facebook: Joel Odunayo Daramola

Websites: www.visionlink4u.com

www.ingramcontent.com/pod-product-compliance
Lightning Source LLC
LaVergne TN
LVHW012115170826
845678LV00014BA/2947

9798369636596